THE LONDON STAGE
1660-1700

A Critical Introduction

THE
LONDON STAGE
1660-1700

A Critical Introduction

BY

Emmett L. Avery

AND

Arthur H. Scouten

SOUTHERN ILLINOIS UNIVERSITY PRESS

CARBONDALE AND EDWARDSVILLE

FEFFER & SIMONS, INC.

LONDON AND AMSTERDAM

ARCTURUS BOOKS EDITION, DECEMBER 1968
COPYRIGHT © 1968 BY SOUTHERN ILLINOIS UNIVERSITY PRESS
ALL RIGHTS RESERVED
LIBRARY OF CONGRESS CATALOG CARD NUMBER 60-6539
THIS EDITION PRINTED BY OFFSET LITHOGRAPHY
IN THE UNITED STATES OF AMERICA
DESIGNED BY ANDOR BRAUN

FOREWORD

THE LONDON STAGE, 1660–1800, now completed in eleven volumes, has resulted from a co-operative scholarly venture lasting for thirty-three years. The five authors have called upon aid from dozens of specialists in the field, and from the staffs of many a library to compile the day-by-day account of what went on upon the London stage, including the booths at fairs and the opera houses, for a hundred-and-forty-year period. Each has acknowledged his debt in the Preface to his own part.

The basic compilation provides the reader with factual and revisitable evidence in strict chronological order as to dates, plays, casts, facilities, scenes, costumes, theatrical management, specialty acts, music, dance, box receipts, and hundreds of illuminating items from contemporary comments in letters, journals, diaries, pamphlets, periodicals, and newspapers. The headnotes to each year tell of the composition of the acting companies, summarize forthcoming theatrical events, and suggest trends and novelties as well as the proportions of tragedy, comedy, history, and musicals to be presented.

Since the eleven-volume reference work may be too massive for individuals to possess, the authors now make available, in this series of five paperbacks, their Critical Introductions to each part. These are both factual and interpretive. Interpretations of identical basic material will, of course, vary as the years go on and as each up-coming stage historian brings to bear upon it his own predilections and interests. The authors, however, planned from the beginning to give the results of their own insights gained from searching out the details, organizing the facts, and living with the fragments of evidence for over a quarter of a century apiece.

Dr. Van Lennep, who undertook the difficult period embraced in Part 1, died before it was completed. The Critical Introduction for that period was prepared by professors Avery and Scouten, who were helping him with the calendar of events for the Restoration era.

The authors hope that these introductions will serve all readers interested in stage history. Each volume deals fully with theatrical events recorded in the blocks of time indicated. Together they tell the cumulative story of a flow of activities dominated by the manager-actor-dramatists who characterized each period—Davenant and Betterton, Cibber, Fielding and Rich, Garrick, and Sheridan and Kemble. All readers are referred for details to the full documentation presented in the complete calendar.

G. W. S., Jr.

New York University
21 April 1968

CONTENTS

THE LONDON STAGE
1660-1700

The Theatrical World, 1660-1700: A General View

RARELY does an art form have its professional development interrupted for a generation. In some respects, however, this happened to the public theatres in London from the prohibition against acting passed late in 1642 by the Commonwealth[1] to the restoration of the monarchy in 1660. For twenty years the Commonwealth, opposed in principle and practice to theatrical entertainments, kept the playhouses under relatively tight rein and frequently reduced acting in the public theatres so severely as to make financially unprofitable the operations of a company and the composing of plays for public presentation. Although plays did not wholly disappear from the stage, the eighteen years from 1642 to 1660 represent an unusual hiatus in the public practice of the various forms of dramatic art, a situation especially unusual for a country which in the preceding century had had a glorious dramatic renaissance.

With the restoration of Charles II early in 1660, an opportunity arose for the theatrical world to begin anew and the player, manager, playwright, and spectator to restore the drama to its former position in England's culture. By 1660 the principal actors of the days of James I and Charles I had died or had so drifted out of touch with dramatic enterprise that the continuity of acting had been impaired, though certainly not lost. Furthermore, most of the pre-Commonwealth theatres had been closed, destroyed, or converted

---

[1] See Leslie Hotson, *The Commonwealth and Restoration Stage* (Cambridge, Mass., 1928), pp. 5-6.

to purposes other than theatrical. In addition, the playwrights of the old regime no longer were productive. And a new generation had appeared in London, one which had little intimate knowledge of acting, the drama, or the playhouse. One can note this frame of mind in Samuel Pepys, who in 1660 and for some years later found the reopened theatrical scene a dazzling sight and who occasionally mentioned, as though it was interesting but not exceptional, taking to the theatre a friend who had never before seen a staged play and was therefore vague concerning the traditions of the drama. During the Commonwealth the drama had not, of course, been extinguished, for old plays had been given (sometimes in public, often in private) and new ones, such as Sir William Davenant's operatic works, had been composed and staged. Nevertheless, the professional theatre, experienced actors, and knowledgeable spectators had to be re-created. In bringing the theatre to life again, the managers, playwrights, performers, and the public developed after 1660 many practices, including some striking innovations, which set the pattern for the London professional theatres for the next hundred and fifty years.

Although it is difficult to determine the relative importance of the innovations and alterations, it is not difficult to select those which had important effects upon the English stage to the end of the eighteenth century: (1) The creation of a monopoly of theatrical enterprises, ordinarily restricted to two patent companies, sometimes compressed into a single company; (2) the introduction of women to act upon the stage, altering the old custom of the boy actor in female roles; (3) the altered design of the playhouses, with the development of the pit as a main seating area, the stage-boxes, front-boxes, and side-boxes as the more expensive and, theoretically, more desirable locations, and the first and second galleries for less expensive tastes; (4) the greatly increased use of scenes, especially changeable scenery, and machines, with an accompanying emphasis upon spectacle in both dramatic and operatic productions; (5) an increasing enlargement of the day's program by means of entr'acte entertainments of singing and dancing, accompanied by a correspondingly greater emphasis in the public concert halls upon vocal and instrumental music. During the forty years from 1660 and 1700 and during most of the eighteenth century, these practices, both singly and in unison, had extremely important effects upon the course of English drama and stagecraft.

Although the first of these events—the creation of a two-company monopoly—apparently came about without extended discussion of the wisdom of a theatrical monopoly, it did not materialize without opposition.

Because the continuity of management had been interrupted by the Common-wealth, a mild scramble for power occurred in 1659 and 1660. The energy and prestige of two men, Sir William Davenant and Thomas Killigrew, as well as their access to Charles II's ear, gave them an exceptional opportunity to secure exclusive rights to form companies and to present plays. At first, however, they were opposed by John Rhodes, Michael Mohun, and William Beeston, theatrical entrepreneurs who wished to form their own companies, and by Sir Henry Herbert, who, as Master of the Revels, opposed the grants to Davenant and Killigrew not because he objected to a monopoly in principle but because he desired that all grants be put directly under his control. Within a short time Davenant and Killigrew won the struggle against other competitors by securing patents to form a monopoly of two companies, and they succeeded in securing considerable, though not com-plete, independence of the Office of the Revels. Although legal measures had to be taken occasionally to suppress upstart companies and although some leniency was allowed to a series of Nurseries for relatively untrained actors, control by Davenant and Killigrew rapidly became effective. The Duke's Company and the King's Company, the names by which these groups were familiarly known, dominated London's theatrical enterprises; and when they had erected two new theatres, Dorset Garden and the Theatre Royal in Bridges Street, they made it virtually impossible for any other company to achieve equality in London. The patent houses strengthened their control by securing regulations which prevented an actor from exercising easy freedom of movement from one position to another.

Nevertheless, monopoly by two companies did not necessarily guarantee financial success. By 1682 the King's Company, weakened by internal dissensions, misfortunes (including the burning of the Bridges Street playhouse a few years earlier), and poor patronage, made overtures to the Duke's Company to form a united enterprise. This amalgamation, essentially an absorption of the weaker King's by the more powerful Duke's Company, exercised until 1695 a virtually unchallenged control over the-atrical offerings. In the season of 1694–95, however, fresh internal dissension caused a secession by the best actors, with the result that from 1695 to the close of the century London again had two companies. This pattern—a two-company structure altering to a single-company monopoly—occurred again in the early years of the next century. In fact, the kinds of monopoly established in 1660 and 1661 set the pattern for limiting the number of legally-operating theatrical companies to two for a great many decades, with the exception of several seasons in the first third of the eighteenth century, when the authorities closed their eyes to violations of this principle. The Licensing Act of 1737 restored a rigorous legalization of a two-company monopoly of dramatic offerings in the regular winter season.

A second innovation, the admission of women to act in the public theatres, also occurred within a year after the reopening of the playhouses in 1660. No doubt, the employment of actresses would have come about in due time as a result of social change, but the interruption in dramatic continuity provided both a stimulus and an occasion. For a very brief time the play-houses retained the employment of boy actors for female roles: for example, Edward Kynaston, William Betterton, and James Nokes. Nevertheless, the dissolution of the repertory companies during the Commonwealth had inhibited the training of boys as female impersonators at the same time that the sojourn of the English court in France had demonstrated the practicality of having women perform upon the stage. Andrew Newport, writing to Sir Richard Leveson upon the new practices in London, 15 December 1660, reflected the influence of the Continent: "Upon our stages we have women actors, as beyond seas."[2] In fact, by the early autumn of 1660, during the formation of the patent houses, a petition (13 October 1660) indicates that the companies had in prospect the engaging of women.[3] We do not know just when the first actress played a major role or who she was, but a woman certainly acted Desdemona in *Othello* in late 1660.[4] Thereafter, although the stage was not a proper place for proper young gentlewomen, many actresses gained recognition and fame—Nell Gwyn is a shining example—even if, in the words of John Downes, prompter to the Duke's Company, they often "by force of Love were Erept the Stage."[5]

The impact of the introduction of actresses is immeasurable. Early in the 1660's it was argued that their presence in the companies would improve the moral tone of the playhouses and the drama. In the patent issued to Killigrew, 25 April 1662, the argument runs as follows:

for as much as many playes formerly acted doe conteine severall prophane, obscene, and scurrulous passages, and the women's part therein have byn acted by men in the habit of women, at which some have taken offence, for the preventing of these abuses for the future . . . wee doe likewise permit and give leave, that all the woemen's

---

[2] HMC, Fifth Report, Part I (1876), p. 158.

[3] Hotson, *Commonwealth and Restoration Stage*, p. 204. See also *The Dramatic Records of Sir Henry Herbert*, ed. J. Q. Adams (New Haven, 1917), pp. 94–96, where a petition by several actors states that they "had by covenant obliged [themselves] to act with woemen."

[4] For a comprehensive account of Restoration actresses, see John Harold Wilson, *All the King's Ladies* (Chicago, 1958).

[5] *Roscius Anglicanus*, ed. Montague Summers (London, n.d.), p. 35.

part . . . may be performed by woemen soe long as their recreacones, which by reason of the abuses aforesaid were scandalous and offensive, may by such reformation be esteemed not onely harmless delight, but useful and instructive.[6]

That this pious hope was not fully realized requires no demonstration, for numerous commentators deplored the private and public lives of the actresses and the fact that the immoral tone of the stage was not genuinely improved by the presence of women. John Evelyn, for example, frequently referred in his diary to the corrupting influences of actresses upon the Court. (See his strongly-worded disapproval in the entry for 18 October 1666.) On the other hand, the delight with which Pepys followed the acting and careers of such actresses as Nell Gwyn and Mary Knepp testifies to the pleasure as well as to the more effective acting which the abilities of women brought to the stage. The actresses, nevertheless, did not fully achieve equality in position, for among the early sharing groups there are no women sharers, although in 1695 actresses and actors became equal sharers in a new company. In numbers, also, the proportion of actors to actresses usually was at least two to one, although this inequality reflected primarily the needs of the companies, as the number of male to female roles in most plays was a disproportionate one. On the other hand, by the end of the seventeenth century the London theatres had trained several women of considerable talent and great proficiency: Nell Gwyn, Katherine Corey, Mary Saunderson Betterton, Frances Knight, Elinor Leigh, Anne Bracegirdle, Elizabeth Barry, and Susanna Percival Mountfort Verbruggen. These women established the actress as an integral part of English theatrical enterprises.

Another result of the long closure of the theatres was an alteration in the physical accommodations. When acting resumed, not all of the older theatres were available, although the old Cockpit in Drury Lane sufficed for awhile. Temporarily, Gibbons' Tennis Court, constructed much earlier, was converted into a not wholly satisfactory playhouse. In these circumstances, both the Duke's and King's companies early planned to build new theatres, and these new structures set the characteristic features of the playhouses for several generations. First of all, the principal new ones—the two in Drury Lane and the theatre in Dorset Garden—were of moderate size, permitting an intimate atmosphere. The stage extended in front of the proscenium arch into the pit, which was fitted with benches (backless), continuing the growing practice of seating nearly all of the spectators and eliminating the large proportion of standees which had been characteristic of some earlier playhouses. Extending from the stage on both sides of the pit

---

[6] See Percy Fitzgerald, *A New History of the English Stage* (London, 1882), I, 80.

were tiers of boxes, commonly referred to as stage-boxes (often a double tier); side boxes (those extending along both sides of the interior); and front-boxes (those facing or fronting the stage, at the rear of the pit). Rising above the front boxes and pit was a gallery or (in some theatres) a lower gallery as well as a smaller upper one. With benches rather than individual seats as the prevailing mode, particularly in the pit, the playhouses had a flexible rather than a fixed capacity. If the performance was sparsely attended, spectators might sit comfortably upon the benches; but if the attendance was very large, the increase was accommodated in part by crowding. At all times, in spite of a tendency for the socially or financially elite to sit apart from those of lesser quality, the spectators talked and listened in an atmosphere of conviviality, as Pepys makes abundantly clear in many entries in his diary. These types of accommodation and the informal, intimate atmosphere essentially prevailed until, in the second half of the eighteenth century, the proprietors embarked upon a steady enlargement of the playhouses, an alteration which affected not only the cohesion of the audience but also its relationship to the actors on stage.

Another change in the technical operations of the playhouses was a vastly increased emphasis upon changeable scenery and devices ("machines") for creating such special effects as flyings of persons and objects. Much of the impetus for this movement came from the imagination and ingenuity of Sir William Davenant, who, some years before the restoration of Charles II, had envisioned public theatres with elaborate embellishments to the action. Although he had experimented in this vein in a few productions during the five years preceding 1660, he lacked a genuine opportunity to develop his theories until he secured a patent and formed a company to act in Lincoln's Inn Fields.[7] John Downes, prompter to Davenant's company, stressed these innovations when he described the opening of that theatre (probably on 28 June 1661) with *The Siege of Rhodes*, an operatic work "having new Scenes and Decorations, being the first that e're were Introduc'd in England."[8] Pepys' first glimpse of this play (2 July 1661) much impressed him, for he found the opening "indeed is very fine and magnificent." By the summer of 1662 Davenant's reliance upon these devices was sufficiently on record that a poem characterizing recent dramatic events referred to the progress of this theatre, "Where the Knight with his Scenes doth keep much adoe."[9]

7 For a full discussion of the history of scenes in the English theatres, see Richard Southern, *Changeable Scenery: Its Origin and Development in the British Theatre* (London, 1952). See also a section on scenes, machines, and properties later in this essay.

8 *Roscius Anglicanus*, p. 20.

9 Hotson, *Commonwealth and Restoration Stage*, p. 246.

Davenant constantly improved his stock of scenery, and although the King's Company, Davenant's rival, somewhat slowly followed his lead, within ten years both companies had invested large sums in this phase of their operations and had set the London theatres upon a venture leading to more and more elaborate and costly creations. Although Davenant did not live to see the new theatre in Dorset Garden which his company constructed, he would have been delighted with the attention given to settings and contrivances in this elegant playhouse. As was true of other innovations, there was no turning back from Davenant's pioneering; thereafter, for many decades, the companies vied with each other in colorful scenes, startling machines, realistic properties and embellishments to the dramas and entr'acte entertainments. In fact, they occasionally praised their own initiative, as did the speaker in the Second Prologue to Shadwell's revision of *The Tempest*, 1674:

> *Had we not for ye pleasure found new wayes*
> *You still had rusty Arras had, & thredbare playes;*
> *Nor Scenes nor Woomen had they had their will,*
> *But some with grizl'd Beards had acted Woomen still.*

Alterations in the daily program accompanied these changes. Possessing increasingly elaborate gear, the management placed greater emphasis upon spectacle. Although the play remained the center of the day's offerings, spectacular staging provided a drawing attraction. Shakespeare's *The Tempest*, for example, owed much of its popularity to its transformation into a dramatic opera or musical drama in which flyings, sinkings, and machines augmented the appeal. Each burst of applause for an operatic spectacle, even if sometimes the receipts did not equal the large expenses, caused the rival companies to launch still more expensive productions. In addition, these spectacles stimulated a taste for musical and terpsichorean novelties, and the managements larded many comedies and even some tragedies with songs, dances, and "vocal and instrumental entertainments," some of which, though not all, were thematically related to the action. The fresh faces, engaging talents, and novelty of actresses popularized these augmentations. Pepys, for example, often expressed his delight in the singing and dancing of Nell Gwyn and Mary Knepp, sometimes being so engrossed by them that he failed to mention his response to the play proper; he occasionally found the incidental music so ravishing that he secured a copy of it for his own collection. Further proof of the drawing power of this new trend appears in the Preface to Thomas Shadwell's *The Humorists* (10 December 1670), where he credits the triumph of his play over its enemies to the delightful dancing of Mrs Johnson, whose talents drew both friends and foes and silenced the loud critics. By the end of the century the newspaper announcements make it evident that song and dance as entr'acte entertainments had begun to assume the dominant position which they were to make secure in the first half of the eighteenth century.

Paralleling this interest in spectacle and music within the playhouses was a steady increase in public concerts as well as operatic works produced at Court. In the 1670's John Bannister, composer-musician, initiated a series of concerts in his "Musick School" and ambitiously intended to offer an hour's program every afternoon except Sunday. Although his success was not immediately sensational, other composers and musicians within a few years imitated him. Steadily the vogue of public concerts increased until, at the end of the century, London had its own center for the performing arts, York Buildings, a concert hall which served for musical entertainments for many decades. To these concerts and to the musical dramas within the theatres the principal composers—John Bannister, Henry Purcell, Daniel Purcell, John Eccles—contributed their talents, and following the dissolution of the United Company each playhouse had, in effect, its resident composer: John Eccles at Lincoln's Inn Fields,[10] Daniel Purcell at Drury Lane. The popularity of songs, overtures, and act-tunes shows in numerous collections, such as *Choice Ayres and Songs*, which, printing both words and music, appeared at regular intervals and offered the public a great proportion of the music presented in the theatres. The most complete catalogue of these[11] lists hundreds of titles or first lines of songs, the great majority deriving from plays or the concert halls.

These characteristics of the theatres and musical halls formed part of the pattern for the next hundred years. In addition, some factors somewhat peculiar to the years from 1660 to 1700 affected the theatres. One was royal patronage, direct and indirect. It was highly influential in the reign of Charles II, for the monarch created and sustained the two-company monopoly, and he lent his royal presence and financial assistance to productions. The monarchical influence was less important in the short reign of James II, occasionally decisive under William and Mary. The authority of these rulers was also of prime importance in protecting managers and playwrights from forces inimical to the stage, for there remained in London a strong anti-stage

10 See Stoddard Lincoln, "Eccles and Congreve: Music and Drama on the Restoration Stage," *Theatre Notebook*, XVIII (1963), 7-18.

11 C. L. Day and E. B. Murrie, *English Song Books 1651-1702* (London, 1940).

sentiment. This undercurrent appears frequently in the comments of John Evelyn, who often incorporated into his journal not only a report of his attendance at a play but coupled with it a strong statement lamenting the gross licentiousness of the stage, drama, and performers. Especially revealing is a long reflection he entered in his Diary after seeing *Mustapha* at Court on 18 October 1666.

This night was acted my Lord Brahals Tragedy cal'd *Mustapha* before their Majesties &c: at Court; at which I was present, very seldom at any time, going to the publique Theaters, for many reasons, now as they were abused, to an atheisticall liberty, fowle & undecent; Women now (& never 'til now) permitted to appeare & act, which inflaming severall young noble-men & gallants . . . & another greater person than any of these, who fell into their snares, to the reproch of their noble families, & ruine both of body & Soule.

Because a strong residue of anti-stage sentiment remained from the Commonwealth era, nearly everyone concerned with the playhouses gave at least lip service to the avoidance of "prophane, obscene, and scurrilous" passages. In the section, already quoted, of Killigrew's patent, the text, for example, asserted the hope that the presence of women in the casts of plays would lessen the ribaldry and licentiousness of the theatres. During the reign of Charles II the support of the monarch was usually sufficient to protect the companies from the severest consequences of an attack by moralists, but that was not true of plays which had dangerous political overtones and implications. In this respect the playhouses suffered most acutely in the years, roughly from 1678 to 1682, when the Popish Plot and the tension provoked by it were at their height. During this period the authorities interdicted several plays: Crowne's *Henry VI, Part I*, Lee's *Lucius Junius Brutus*, Tate's *Richard II*, Dryden-Lee's *The Duke of Guise*, and Crowne's *The City Politiques*. The vagaries of the political temper sometimes made Dryden's *The Spanish Fryar* acceptable, at other times unacceptable. Under a less tolerant and less powerful ruler, the hazards of the political and moral antagonisms might have been the undoing of the theatres.

In the late years of the century, the playhouses came under much more vigorous attack from the moralists, who secured indictments against several players for speaking licentious or blasphemous lines, an action not typical of the reign of Charles II. The most powerful essays against the stage appeared in the writings of Jeremy Collier and the activities of the Societies for the Reformation of Manners. The publication of Collier's *A Short View of the Immorality and Profaneness of the English Stage* in 1698 was a shocking revelation of the strong antagonism existing outside the Court and literary circles; it had lively support from the clergy, some men of letters, the citizenry, and the authorities. The strength of Collier's documentation of dramatic licentiousness, according to his conceptions of licence, dismayed the dramatists, who sometimes replied intemperately and, without so intending, encouraged other pamphleteers to join the crusade against the playhouses. The number of prosecutions of actors after 1698 for uttering licentious expressions testifies to the efforts of the authorities to make an issue of the conflict between the stage and morality. Although the attacks by Collier and his followers did not destroy the stage, they placed it on the defensive; and in 1698, 1699, and 1700 the companies lacked a strong monarch (like Charles II) willing to defend them against a powerful animus. Not only did the companies stand in danger of persecution, but the temper of the times altered the course of the drama, a trend exemplified in the withdrawal of a playwright with the stature of William Congreve, who composed no major plays after 1700, and in the increasingly sentimental tone of English comedy.

All in all, there are few periods in the history of the English stage when so many important changes occurred within the span of a generation and a half. It was an exciting age. The theatres were restored to an important place in the entertainment of the populace at large and the Court. Innovations of great influence upon succeeding theatrical enterprises made their appearance. The playwrights added a large number of new plays which were to become standard fare in the repertories of the next century, and a moderately large number of these plays, especially the comedies, have endured into modern times as brilliant stage fare. And the age produced several capable, even brilliant, performers whose names have not lost their lustre with the passage of time: Thomas Betterton, Nell Gwyn, Anne Bracegirdle, Elizabeth Barry.

The Playhouses

EVEN before the return of Charles II to the throne was a certainty, several theatrical entrepreneurs had undertaken to present plays or had prepared to do so as promptly as was legal or feasible. As a result, for several years a number of companies played in several theatres, some improvised from structures basically nontheatrical, others in playhouses surviving from the pre-Commonwealth era, and still others in new structures created by the patent companies under the management of Sir William Davenant and Thomas Killigrew. The following pages offer a brief account of the history, location, basic accommodations, and distinguishing characteristics of each playhouse in the approximate order of its first use following the end of the Commonwealth. These descriptions conclude with a brief statement concerning other places of entertainment, such as the Fairs and concert halls.

THE RED BULL THEATRE

One of the older theatres which served briefly for dramatic performances at the Restoration was the Red Bull. This house, which had been built on land leased by Aron Holland in Elizabethan times,[12] stood at the upper end of St John Street in the parish of St James, Clerkenwell. By 1653 the playhouse had been rebuilt and enlarged.[13] According to *Historia Histrionica* (1699), the theatre lay partly open to the weather,[14] and although it has been argued that by 1660 the building had been roofed over, Hotson doubts that this alteration occurred, for he cites the cost and physical difficulty of placing a heavy roof upon the superstructure.[15]

Sometime before the return of Charles II was little more than a hope, Anthony Turner and Edward Shatteral had been ordered (12 May 1659) to appear before the Middlesex Sessions for unlawfully acting at the Red

---

[12] Hotson, *Commonwealth and Restoration Stage*, p. 82.
[13] *Ibid.*, p. 86.
[14] Reprinted in Cibber's *Apology*, ed. R. W. Lowe (London, 1888), I, xxix.
[15] *Commonwealth and Restoration Stage*, p. 87.

Bull.[16] During the summer of 1660 a theatrical company, about which little is known, occupied this house, for Pepys attended a performance there on 3 August 1660. In the season of 1660–61 players again occupied it, Pepys attending at least once and seeing *All's Lost by Lust* on 23 March 1660/1. Performances continued in the season of 1661–62, for on 22 January 1661/2 Jacques Thierry and Will Schellinks, two foreign visitors, saw a play entitled *The New Made Nobleman*.[17] Sometime between then and the summer of 1663 acting apparently ceased at the Red Bull, for in the first act of Davenant's *A Play-House to be Lett* (ca. August 1663) two fencers are informed that now only fencing masters occupy the Red Bull. For example, a "Trial of Skill," presumably an exercise in physical dexterity, took place there on 30 May 1664.[18]

Probably the Red Bull did not survive the Great Fire of 1666. Not much is known concerning its physical characteristics. If it remained un-roofed after the Restoration, with performances subject to the vagaries of the weather, it could not successfully have competed with the new, enclosed theatres constructed after 1660. On a visit to it on 23 March 1660/1 Pepys refers to a tiring room, a music room, and the pit; he also paints a rather sorry picture of it as a functioning playhouse: "where I was led by a seaman that knew me, but is here as a servant, up to the tireing-room, where strange the confusion and disorder that there is among them in fitting themselves, especially here, where the clothes are very poor, and the actors but common fellows."[19]

THE COCKPIT, DRURY LANE

Another of the older theatres available in 1660 was that known in Pepys' day as the Cockpit in Drury Lane. Its origins lying in Elizabethan times, it had been sometimes referred to as The Phoenix but more commonly as the Cockpit.[20] In late 1609 John Best built this theatre as one of a series of buildings upon a site in the parish of St Giles in the Fields,[21] and in 1616 Christopher Beeston hired it from Best at an annual rental of £45, the lease

[16] *Middlesex County Records*, ed. J. C. Jeaffreson (London, 1886–92), III, 279.

[17] Ethel Seaton, *Literary Relations of England and Scandinavia in the Seventeenth Century* (Oxford, 1935), pp. 333–35.

[18] William Van Lennep, "The Death of the Red Bull," *Theatre Notebook*, XVI (1962), 133–34.

[19] For full accounts of the history of the Red Bull, see J. Q. Adams, *Shakespearean Playhouses* (Boston, 1917), pp. 294–309; Hotson *Commonwealth and Restoration Stage*, pp. 82–87; and Van Lennep, "The Death of the Red Bull," pp. 126–34.

[20] Adams, *Shakespearean Playhouses*, pp. 348–49.

[21] Hotson, *Commonwealth and Restoration Stage*, p. 88.

to run thirty-one years from 29 September 1616.[22] The Cockpit buildings comprised an area charted by Drury Lane, Great Queen Street, Great Wild Street, and Prince's Street.[23] According to *Historia Histrionica* (1699),[24] it was not essentially different from Blackfriars and Salisbury Court; like the latter, it was of brick construction.[25] When it opened in 1617, it was under the management of Christopher Beeston, but by 1649 John Rhodes apparently had acquired it by lease.[26] In 1658 Sir William Davenant produced there his operatic work, *The Siege of Rhodes*.

In 1659, according to Downes,[27] Rhodes had a company acting at the Cockpit, and on 4 February 1659/60 Thomas Lilleston was charged with unlawfully performing there. Although Rhodes received a fine for illegal playing on 28 July 1660, Pepys saw *The Loyal Subject* there on 18 August 1660. By 8 October 1660 Killigrew and Davenant had agreed to put their united company into the Cockpit.[28] As this union lasted, however, for only a few weeks, the theatre then lost its importance as a Restoration playhouse.[29]

SALISBURY COURT PLAYHOUSE

Another older theatre available in 1660 was the Salisbury Court Playhouse. Its origins lie in the summer of 1629 when Richard Gunnell, an actor, and William Blagrove, a Deputy to the Master of the Revels, contracted to build a playhouse on land leased from the Earl of Dorset in the Parish of St. Bridges at the lower end of Salisbury Court. The lease, to run forty-one and one-half years, was signed on 6 July 1629 and specified the site as a plot 140 feet in length, 42 in width.[30] The author of *Historia Histrionica* (1699) called it a small house, comparable to Blackfriars or the Cockpit,[31] but Adams believes that it may have been smaller than either of those two theatres.[32]

[22] *Ibid.*, p. 89.

[23] *Ibid.*, pp. 90–91. See also Adams, *Shakespearean Playhouses*, p. 348, and the map opposite page 350.

[24] In Cibber's *Apology*, I, xxviii–xxix.

[25] Adams, *Shakespearean Playhouses*, p. 350.

[26] Hotson, *Commonwealth and Restoration Stage*, p. 99.

[27] *Roscius Anglicanus*, p. 17.

[28] Adams, *Shakespearean Playhouses*, p. 366.

[29] For further details of the history of the Cockpit in Drury Lane, see Adams, *Shakespearean Playhouses*, pp. 348–67, and Hotson, *Commonwealth and Restoration Stage*, pp. 88–100.

[30] Adams, *Shakespearean Playhouses*, pp. 368–72.

[31] In Cibber's *Apology*, I, xxviii–xxix.

[32] Adams, *Shakespearean Playhouses*, p. 373.

In a complaint brought by William Beeston, 25 June 1658, the original cost was given as £1500.[33] During the Commonwealth a company of soldiers dismantled the interior, and for several years preceding 1658 Beeston engaged in litigation to secure his claim to the building through the lease granted in 1629. By 1659, in anticipation of the return of the monarchy, he had renovated the structure,[34] and at the Restoration he had it under rental. During this time he proposed to alter the structure by erecting a room for a dancing school (forty foot square), repairing all the seats and boxes, and raising the roof by thirty feet. The litigation also refers to the existence of galleries.[35] Eventually the plan for the dancing room was altered to allow eight small rooms. Unfortunately, the sight lines to the upper area were such that spectators in the second row could not see the actors on the stage.[36]

The date of the first acting at Salisbury Court after the Restoration is not certain, but the authorities apparently issued a license in June 1660.[37] Although 5 November 1660 (see the Calendar) has been proposed as the probable day of reopening this theatre, the first certain performance occurred on 29 January 1660/1. Davenant did not long occupy this house, for in June 1661 he moved to his new one, Lisle's Tennis Court in Lincoln's Inn Fields. During the summer of 1661 George Jolly occupied Salisbury Court, and in August 1663 and September 1664[38] the authorities ordered the apprehension of William Beeston for acting there without a license. The Great Fire of 1666 destroyed the structure.

VERE STREET THEATRE

This theatre, one of those created primarily for the newly formed Restoration companies, was made suitable for theatrical entertainments by a reconstruction of Gibbons' Tennis Court, one of the more famous of its kind. The structure had its main entrance on Vere Street, the site being near Clare Market and Lincoln's Inn Fields. It was here, Hotson believes,[39] that Sir William Davenant presented his entertainments in 1658. But with

33 Hotson, *Commonwealth and Restoration Stage*, p. 100.
34 *Ibid.*, pp. 101, 106, 108.
35 *Ibid.*, pp. 108–9.
36 *Ibid.*, pp. 112–13.
37 Herbert, *Dramatic Records*, p. 81.
38 Hotson, *Commonwealth and Restoration Stage*, p. 114. For further details concerning the history of this theatre, see Adams, *Shakespearean Playhouses*, pp. 368–83; Hotson pp. 100–114; and the Calendar.
39 Hotson, *Commonwealth and Restoration Stage*, p. 146.

the establishment of two new companies (the King's and the Duke's) in 1660, it was Thomas Killigrew, directing the King's Company, who installed his actors in this newly-renovated house in November 1660. He remained there until 7 May 1663. During those years he constructed a new Theatre Royal in Bridges Street, Drury Lane. Shortly after Killigrew left Vere Street, Pepys, on 1 June 1663, walking in the neighborhood, noted that the building had been used for fencing matches. Still later, on 13 June 1663, a Noncomformist minister preached from the stage to his congregation seated in the pit and boxes.[40]

For the next few years little is known of activities there, but Mrs Pepys, on 23 April 1669, reported to her husband that she had attended a play at the New Nursery, now established in the Vere Street Theatre. Thereafter the edifice lost its status as an active playhouse.[41]

LISLE'S TENNIS COURT, LINCOLN'S INN FIELDS

This playhouse, converted from a tennis court, as was the Vere Street Theatre, had a highly important share in the stagecraft of the early Restoration period, for it was here that Davenant first used in a professional theatre movable and changeable scenery.[42] The origins of the tennis court lie in the winter of 1656–57, when Anne Tyler, whose husband was Thomas Lisle, and James Hooker developed the structure. According to Hotson's conjectures, the tennis court was about seventy-five feet long, thirty feet wide.

In March 1660 Davenant contracted for a lease of the building, in order to convert it into a theatre. Needing more room, he leased adjoining land and structures. (See the drawings in Hotson, opposite pages 122 and 124.) The conversion and the enlargement of the site occupied Davenant until June 1661, when, probably on June 28 (see the Calendar), he opened with *The Siege of Rhodes*. Downes, his prompter, emphasized the historic importance of the occasion: "new Scenes and Decorations, being the first that e're were introduc'd in England" (pp. 20–21).

The Duke's Company occupied the theatre until 9 November 1671, when the company moved to its wholly new playhouse in Dorset Garden. It was probably dark until after the burning of the Theatre Royal in Bridges Street (January 1672), when Killigrew took his orphaned King's Company

[40] See British Museum, Add. MSS 31916, fol. 104.

[41] For a full account of this structure, both as a tennis court and as a playhouse, see Hotson, *Commonwealth and Restoration Stage*, pp. 114–20, 146–47, 177, 189.

[42] For its history, see Hotson, pp. 120–27.

there and occupied it until he could build a new Theatre Royal in Drury
Lane. After 26 March 1674, when Killigrew opened his new house, the
structure in Lincoln's Inn Fields again became a tennis court. Yet once more,
in 1695, it was remodeled into a playhouse, this time to house the company
formed by Thomas Betterton. In this form it endured into the next century.

THE COURT THEATRES

The Restoration Court Stage has been the subject of a full study in a book
with that title.43 It is, therefore, necessary here to give only a brief summary
of the principal facts concerning the theatres created for entertainments
at Court.

At the Restoration the Cockpit in Whitehall was available for acting
but in need of repairs. The renovations began as early as November 1660
(p. 14), and the first performance, a presentation of *The Silent Woman* on
19 November 1660, probably occurred in a room not fully remodeled. This
theatre continued to be utilized to the end of 1664 (p. 19).

Of much greater importance to Court performances was the construction of the Hall Theatre in 1665. Probably planned and certainly constructed
by John Webb (p. 27), it had interior dimensions of 39½ by 87 feet (p. 29).
The stage had a depth of 32 or 33 feet, being 5 feet high alongside the pit
(p. 30), which comprised the space between the stage and the King's dais
(pp. 30–31). The Hall Theatre also had a gallery (p. 32).

This theatre was presumably ready in the late spring of 1665, but the
Great Plague permitted only a few productions before the Court left London
on 29 June 1665. After the Plague, the first known performance of a play
there was *Wit Without Money* on 11 October 1666. The theatre continued
in use until 1698, when it was lost in the fire at Whitehall (p. 56). For
numerous details of the construction, embellishments, repairs, and performances there, see Miss Boswell's study in its entirety.

BRIDGES STREET, DRURY LANE

This theatre, one of a series to bear the distinguished name of Drury Lane,
was initiated on 20 December 1661, when the interested parties signed a

43 Eleanore Boswell, *The Restoration Court Stage* (Cambridge, Mass., 1932). Page references
here are to this Work.

lease and an agreement for its construction.44 To be completed by Christmas 1662, the playhouse was to cost £1500 and to be on a site measuring 112 feet in length, 58 in width. The ground rent was to be £50 annually.45 By 28 January 1661/2 arrangements had been completed for holding the ground in trust for the actors and managers, the whole to be divided into 36 parts, a portion of these to be allotted to the actor-sharers;46 the sharers were to pay the cost of construction at a rate of £3 10s. each acting day.

The theatre opened on 7 May 1663. Although Samuel Pepys did not attend the opening, his account of the second day's performance offers specific details concerning the interior: "The house is made with extraordinary good contrivance, and yet hath some faults, as the narrowness of the passages in and out of the pitt, and the distance from the stage to the boxes, which I am confident cannot hear; but for all other things it is well, only, above all, the musique being below, and most of it sounding under the very stage, there is no hearing of the bases at all, nor very well of the trebles, which sure must be mended." According to S. Sorbière, writing in 1664, the stage was handsomely decorated; he asserted that the best places were in the pit, and he complimented the scenes, the music, and the performers.47 Some years later, 19 October 1667, Pepys, sitting in an upper box, remarked that from this perspective the scenes "do appear very fine indeed, and much better than in the pit." Two years later, on 15 April 1669, Prince Cosmo III of Tuscany, who toured England and saw several plays in the principal theatres, added a few details to Pepys' account: "This theatre is nearly of a circular form, surrounded, in the inside, by boxes separated from each other, and divided into several rows of seats, for the better accommodation of the ladies and gentlemen, who, in conformity with the freedom of the country, sit together indiscriminately; a large space being left on the ground-floor for the rest of the audience."48

The essential features of the theatre appear to have been a pit, sloping somewhat steeply away from the stage, with a tier of boxes on the outer lines of the pit; a second tier, a middle gallery, divided into boxes; and a nondivided gallery above it. The orchestra, as Pepys indicated, occupied an area in front of and below the stage. Following the lead of Sir William

---

44 Allardyce Nicoll, *A History of Restoration Drama 1660–1700*, 4th ed. (Cambridge, 1952), pp. 281–82; Fitzgerald, *A New History*, I, 81–82.

45 Hotson, *Commonwealth and Restoration Stage*, p. 243.

46 Fitzgerald, *A New History*, I, 81–82.

47 *Relation d'un voyage en Angleterre* (Paris, 1664), p. 63, and translated as *A Voyage to England* (London, 1709), pp. 69–71.

48 Conte Lorenzo Magalotti, *The Travels of Cosmo the Third* (London, 1821), p. 191.

Davenant, who had given special attention to scenes, the theatre in Bridges Street also had provisions made for scenes and machines. The playhouse, lighted by candles, may have received some illumination from a cupola at the top, from which, on 1 May 1668, rain dripped onto the spectators, a distraction which, in Pepys' account, created "a disorder in the pit."

The theatre came to a violent end. On 25 January 1671/2, the structure caught fire around eight in the evening and was almost totally destroyed. In addition to the loss of scenes and properties and the injuries sustained by several persons, one member of the company, Richard Bell, lost his life.

THE NURSERIES

During the first two decades following the Restoration, several Nurseries held brief tenures in London, sometimes acting in playhouses abandoned by the principal companies, occasionally playing in temporary or newly designed quarters. Instead of tracing here the complicated history of the various Nurseries, it will suffice to refer briefly to the principal places (other than playhouses treated elsewhere in this section) which housed a Nursery.

HATTON GARDEN. After the re-opening of the theatres at the cessation of the Great Plague, Thomas Killigrew, using a patent which had come into his possession, set up a Nursery in 1667 under Captain Edward Bedford in Hatton Garden.[49] Very little is known of theatrical activities at this location, except that the Nursery remained there until 1668, that James Shirley's *The Constant Maid* was performed, and that Joseph Haines acted with the company, transferring to the King's Company by 7 March 1667/8. By 23 April 1669 the Nursery had abandoned Hatton Garden.[50]

BARBICAN. In the summer of 1671 Lady Davenant planned to erect a playhouse in Barbican to serve as a Nursery, for she presented a petition, on 19 October 1671, seeking permission from the Mayor's Court. The request met with a great deal of opposition,[51] but the enterprise succeeded and lasted for an undetermined number of years, certainly into the next-to-last decade of the seventeenth century.[52]

BUN HILL. In April 1671 John Perin, wishing to build a booth or playhouse, contracted with Thomas Duckworth for the construction of one in Finsbury Fields upon Bun Hill. The building was to be sixty feet long,

49 Hotson, *Commonwealth and Restoration Stage*, p. 188.
50 *Ibid.*, pp. 188–89.
51 *Ibid.*, p. 190.
52 *Ibid.*, pp. 191–94.

forty wide, and to cost £300. Upon completion of the structure, Perin operated the theatre for nine weeks, but nothing is concretely known of the dramatic entertainments he offered. Difficulties arising between Perin and Lady Davenant caused the building to remain empty for a half-year. After Christmas 1671 Duckworth partially dismantled the playhouse.[53]

All of these Nurseries apparently met with considerable disfavor from the City of London and sometimes from the patent companies. Other authorities occasionally threatened their security. On 23 November 1671, for example, Joseph Williamson, the Secretary of State, alarmed at disorders in London, advised the King: "The Nursery in London. Pull down that and coffee houses. If the two nurseries in Barbican and Bunhill be not taken away in a year, expect a disorder. The apprentices are already grown too heady."[54] On the other hand, all of them provided, at the minimum, a means of training and livelihood for young performers. An occasional one, such as Joseph Haines, graduated to the patent companies. Others may have become members of the companies which John Coysh and John Perin formed into strolling companies.

DORSET GARDEN THEATRE

In late 1669 or early 1670 the Duke's Company, created by Sir William Davenant and continuing under the control of the Davenant family, initiated the construction of a new theatre. On 11 August 1670 Roger Jerman leased a piece of ground in Dorset Garden to Henry Harris and John Roffley in trust for Lady Davenant, Thomas Betterton, and other sharers for 39 years from 23 December 1669 at a yearly rental of £130.[55] On 12 August 1670 the sharers agreed to raise £3,000, each contributing in proportion to his share to complete the structure and agreeing to pay more if necessary. According to later testimony, the cost rose to £9,000, the charge being £450 on each of twenty shares. The daily rent (paid to the investors) varied through the years: £5 per acting day from 9 November 1671 to 16 March 1671/2; £6 thereafter to 23 February 1673/4; £7 afterwards.[56] Charles II eased some of the burden of this large expenditure by a gift of £1,000.[57]

53 *Ibid.*, pp. 189–90.
54 *Calendar State Papers Domestic*, Charles II, ccxciv, 64. See also Hotson, *Commonwealth and Restoration Stage*, p. 191.
55 Hotson, *Commonwealth and Restoration Stage*, p. 229.
56 *Ibid.*, pp. 229–32.
57 Aston Papers, British Museum, Add. MSS 36, 916, Vol. XVI, fol. 233.

According to tradition, Sir Christopher Wren designed the building. It fronted the river, its façade decorated with the arms of its patron, James Duke of York. In over-all dimensions the building was 140 feet long, 57 feet wide; the upper story contained apartments, one of them occupied by Thomas Betterton, who often managed the company.[58] Its capacity is not known, but François Brunet, who visited the theatre in 1676, pointed out some of its distinctive features. He reported that the amphitheatre sloped upward toward the boxes. On the lower tier were seven boxes, each seating twenty persons; above these, the middle gallery, divided into seven boxes of equal capacity; and above this portion, the upper gallery. If his calculations are correct, the boxes, lower and middle, would accommodate 280 persons.[59] When John Evelyn, on 28 June 1671, stopped by this theatre, which was not then completed, he was impressed by the magnificence of the scenes and machines. The playhouse opened on 9 November 1671 with John Dryden's *Sir Martin Marall* as the attraction.

For the next ten years the theatre in Dorset Garden fulfilled the needs of the Duke's Company. When it and the King's Company joined in 1682, the United Company had at its disposal both Drury Lane and Dorset Garden. Because the latter was more elaborately equipped for spectacle, the United Company ordinarily presented there such operatic works as *The Prophetess* and *King Arthur*, reserving Drury Lane for drama requiring a more intimate atmosphere. When the United Company dissolved in 1695, Christopher Rich and Sir Thomas Skipwith retained possession of both theatres to the end of the century; but they utilized Dorset Garden less and less frequently. In fact, in the closing years of the century, it served for such spectacles as a lottery and exhibitions of strength and agility by the "Kentish Strong Man." The theatre was demolished in 1709.

A lament for the decline of this proud theatre appeared in the Prologue to *The Constant Couple* (28 November 1699):

> *Ah Friends! poor Dorset-Garden-house is gone;*
> *Our merry Meetings there are all undone:*
> *Quite lost to us, sure for some strange Misdeeds,*
> *That strong Dog Sampson's pull'd it o'er our Heads.*

[58] Hotson, *Commonwealth and Restoration Stage*, pp. 233–34.
[59] *Ibid.*, p. 236.

THEATRE ROYAL, DRURY LANE

Following the fire in January 1672 which destroyed the theatre in Bridges Street occupied by the King's Company, Thomas Killigrew, after establishing his actors temporarily in the old playhouse in Lincoln's Inn Fields, promptly began preparations to construct a new theatre. This was not an easy task. The King's Company had lost nearly all of its resources, except the players, plays, technical knowledge, and determination. Building costs had risen, and the new Duke's Theatre in Dorset Garden had put Killigrew's company at a great disadvantage. The disabled company made an appeal to Charles II for financial aid, but it is not known whether he heeded the request. By contrast, it is ironic that, in view of the opposition of many of the clergy to the stage, one source of funds for building a new Drury Lane was a collection made in parish churches throughout England. For example, a token gift of two shillings came from the church at Berwick and another two shillings from Symonsbury in Dorset.[60]

On 17 December 1673 the sharers of the King's Company entered into articles for the construction of the new playhouse. The costs are not certainly known, but, utilizing comparisons based on the acting day's rent paid to the building investors, Hotson has estimated that the structure cost approximately £4,000, not quite twice the cost of the old Theatre Royal in Bridges Street and not quite half the apparent cost of the new Dorset Garden Theatre. In addition, the Company had to secure scenes and costumes; it also built a scene-house adjoining the theatre. The latter was financed without recourse to the building investors.[61]

The dimensions of the old Theatre Royal had been 112 feet in length by 58 or 59 feet in width. The width of the new remained the same, but the addition of a scene-room increased the length to 140 feet.[62] A brief account of this theatre by Henri Misson, traveling in London in the last decade of the seventeenth century, clarifies some aspects of its structure and appearance.

There are two Theatres at London, one large and handsome [Dorset Garden], where they sometimes act Opera's and sometimes Plays; the other [Drury Lane] something smaller, which is only for Plays. The Pit is an Amphitheatre, fill'd with Benches without Backboards, and adorn'd and cover'd with green Cloth. Men of

---

[60] See *Essex Archeological Collections* (1853), VI, 242, and the R. J. Smith Collection of Dramatic Materials, British Museum, p. 169.

[61] Hotson, *Commonwealth and Restoration Stage*, pp. 254–55.

[62] *Ibid.*, p. 256.

Quality, particularly the younger Sort, some Ladies of Reputation and Vertue, and abundance of Damsels that hunt for Prey, sit all together in this Place, Higgledy-piggledy, chatter, toy, play, hear, hear not. Further up, against the Wall, under the first Gallery, and just opposite to the Stage, rises another Amphitheatre, which is taken up by Persons of the best Quality, among whom are generally very few Men. The Galleries, whereof there are only two Rows, are fill'd with none but ordinary People, particularly in the Upper one.[63]

Among the decorations of the interior were busts or portraits of dramatists, referred to as "the Poets Heads" in the *Epilogue Spoken at the Opening of the New House*, 26 March 1674, and described more fully in Thomas D'Urfey's *Collin's Walk Through London and Westminster* (1690, Canto IV):

> He saw each Box with Beauty crown'd,
> And Pictures deck the Structure round;
> Ben, Shakespear, and the learned Rout,
> With Noses some, and some without.

The theatre opened on 26 March 1674 with *The Beggar's Bush*. A Prologue written by John Dryden for the occasion contrasts this "Plain Built House" and "mean ungilded Stage" with the pomp of Dorset Garden. Nevertheless, both the Prologue and Epilogue bravely argue the merits of the new theatre, its devotion to plays rather than to operatic spectacle and decoration, and pledge a better atmosphere for English drama.[64]

The King's Company acted in Drury Lane until the Union in 1682. Thereafter the United Company occupied it, principally for drama, while continuing to present spectacles at Dorset Garden. By the end of the seventeenth century, particularly after the defection of Thomas Betterton and his associates in 1695, Drury Lane tended to be utilized more frequently than Dorset Garden, with the result that when Christopher Rich and Sir Thomas Skipwith dominated the patent company, Drury Lane supplanted its one-time rival and survived into the eighteenth century as a major London theatre.

The capacity of this playhouses during the two and one-half decades of its use in the seventeenth century is not known, but a few clues exist in two documents recording the receipts there on 12 and 26 December 1677.[65] On the first evening the pit held 117 spectators; on the second, 191. On the first evening the gallery held 63 auditors; on the second, 144. In the

---

[63] *M. Misson's Memoirs and Observations . . . Translated by Mr Ozell* (London, 1719), pp. 219–20.
[64] The Epilogue also argued that "Our House relieves the Ladies from the Frights / Of ill pav'd Street, and long dark Winter Nights."
[65] See Fitzgerald, *A New History*, I, 145, for a reproduction of these receipts.

upper gallery, on the first day, were 33 spectators; on the second, 119. The probable attendance in the boxes on 12 December 1677 was 38 spectators; on 26 December, 60 persons. Since the receipts on 26 December amounted to £52 19s. and since £140 appears to have been one of the largest receipts (and that on a benefit day) during the Restoration, it may be assumed that the approximately 515 spectators present on 26 December represented a moderately profitable house, large enough to leave a small profit after the house charges, which probably fell in the £30 to £35 range at that time. Because of the flexible seating arrangements (benches, not individual seats, in the pit), it is difficult to determine a comfortable capacity, for £140 in receipts would certainly represent a crowded house. It seems likely that a £100 house would be a very good one, perhaps possible without severe crowding. If, then, receipts of £52 19s. represented about 515 spectators, receipts of £100 would represent an audience of about 1,000 spectators.

LINCOLN'S INN FIELDS, 1695–

When Thomas Betterton, Elizabeth Barry, and Anne Bracegirdle, the leaders of the dissenters from the United Company, withdrew to form their own sharing company in the season of 1694–95, they lacked access to a suitable theatre, for the United Company controlled both Drury Lane and Dorset Garden. As a result, in Cibber's words, they resorted to "creating a theatre within the Walls of the Tennis-Court in Lincoln's-Inn-Fields."[66] (See the earlier section on Lisle's Tennis Court, Lincoln's Inn Fields.)

Possessing only limited financial resources, the dissident actors relied upon the goodwill of the town to assist them in an emergency. The town responded, according to Cibber, for, after the company obtained a permit, "many People of Quality came into a voluntary Subscription of twenty, and some of forty Guineas a-piece, for erecting a Theatre."[67] The remodeling was done in some haste, for the company had less than a year in which to alter the interior and prepare scenes, costumes, and properties. The theatre opened in April 1695 with Congreve's *Love for Love* as the initial attraction.

Although the small size of the improvised theatre made it well suited to an intimacy between actor and spectator, the playhouse was, by contrast with Dorset Garden and, possibly, Drury Lane, quite small and poorly equipped for spectacle and operatic productions. In fact, its inadequacy

---

66 *Apology*, I, 194.
67 *Ibid.*

provoked occasional satiric thrusts. For example, the Prologue to *The Fatal Discovery*, acted at the opposition theatre, Drury Lane, probably in February 1698, contemptuously referred to Lincoln's Inn Fields as "Betterton's Booth."

Even so, Betterton's company attempted some elaborate productions. One of these, *Rinaldo and Armida*, seemed so incongruous in such a small theatre that the author of *A Comparison Between the Two Stages* (1702) had a good deal of fun with it.

This surpriz'd not only Drury-Lane, but indeed all the Town, no body ever dreaming of an Opera there; 'tis true they had heard of Homer's Illiads in a Nut-shel, and Jack in a Box, and what not? but where's the wonder? why such amazement? I have seen the Creation of the World, *Alexander*'s Exploit's, *Robin Hood* and *Little John*, and I don't know how much, all epitomiz'd into a Rarre-show, carry'd about on a Man's Head.[68]

In spite of these disadvantages, Betterton and his co-sharers made no attempt to build or otherwise secure a new theatre and they occupied Lincoln's Inn Fields until early in the eighteenth century.

THE FAIRS

During this period three Fairs offered entertainments which, at times, imitated or competed with those presented in the playhouses: Bartholomew, Southwark, and May Fair.[69] Of the three, Bartholomew and Southwark flourished, with occasional interruptions, from 1660 to 1700, whereas May Fair was principally restricted to the closing decade of the century. All three continued into the succeeding century.

BARTHOLOMEW FAIR. Held in the closing days of August, this Fair during the early years following the return of Charles II offered novelties: dancing monkeys, dancing on the ropes, malformed animals (on 4 September 1663 Pepys saw a goose with four feet, a cock with three feet), clock works, puppetry, and a mare that counted money. The puppetry, of course, most closely bordered on the dramatic. Pepys, for example, saw *Patient Grizzill* on 30 August 1667 and *Merry Andrew* (an interlude) on 29 August 1668.

68 Edited by S. B. Wells (Princeton, 1942), p. 22.

69 For an account of Bartholomew Fair throughout its long history, see Henry Morley, *Memoirs of Bartholomew Fair* (London, 1892), and for a full discussion of the theatrical offerings at the three Fairs, see Sybil Rosenfeld, *The Theatre of the London Fairs in the Eighteenth Century* (Cambridge, 1960).

Occasionally a skillful performer, such as Jacob Hall, danced on the ropes and won applause as a specialty artist.

After 1680 records of dramatic works increase. During August 1682 a company, referred to as the Newmarket Company, played *The Irish Evidence* and *The Humours of Tiege; or, The Mercenary Whore*. In the summer of 1692 a performer acted Jack Pudding and was seized for his politically dangerous remarks.[70] In 1694 one Thura, visiting in London, saw *The Unhappy Marriage;* two years later, in the summer of 1696, a Jack Pudding was again arrested for his improvisations on political themes. In 1699 a greater abundance of news concerning theatrical events indicates that a droll called *The Devil of a Wife* was given, and that Parker and Doggett presented at a booth *Fryar Bacon; or, The Country Justice*. In the summer of 1700 the authorities forbade booths for stage plays,[71] and the Fair reverted to its old status of a conglomeration of tumbling, rope dancing, oddities, and exhibitions of dexterities, catering to persons of all classes and tastes.

In addition to the performances listed in the yearly entries for Bartholomew Fair in the Calendar, some extant brills probably represent late seventeenth-century offerings which cannot be more precisely dated.[72] These chiefly advertise songs and dances, agilities and dexterities, and oddities. The following bill offers a typical diversity:

W R

By His Majesty's Permission

At the King's Head on the Paved Stones in West-Smithfield, during the time of Bartholomew-Fair is to be seen.

The Eighth great Wonder of the World, viz. a young-Man about the 24th Year of his Age, who (tho he was born without Arms) performs all manner of Martial Exercises with his Feet: In the first place he beats the Drum and sounds the Trumpet, at one and the same time; he flourishes his Colours, plays at Back-Sword, Charges and Fires a Pistol with great Expedition and Dexterity: He also plays at Cards or Dice, and can also Comb his Head, and Shave his Beard: and does readily pull off his Hat and courteously salutes the Company, he uses a Fork at Meat; and will take a Glass in one Foot and a Glass in the other and so fill the Glass and genteely drink a Health to the Company; Moreover he can thread a Needle, Embroider, and play upon several sorts of Musick; and what is yet more wonderful, writes Six sorts of very fair Hands. He has been but few days in England, but has had the Honour to show

---

[70] Narcissus Luttrell, *A Brief Historical Relation of State Affairs* (Oxford, 1857), III, 176. See also the Newdigate Newsletters (Folger Shakespeare Library).

[71] *Flying Post*, 4–6 July 1700.

[72] See Rosenfeld, *The Theatre of the London Fairs*, p. 8. These bills, in the Harvard Theatre Collection, have been transcribed by Professor A. H. Scouten.

himself before most of the Princes and Princesses of Europe, and may be seen at any time of the Day, without Loss of Time. Vivat Rex.

SOUTHWARK FAIR. Following closely upon the heels of Bartholomew Fair, that in Southwark offered similar, if not identical, entertainments. John Evelyn, for example, on 13 September 1660 saw novelties and dexterities of a kind familiar to devotees of Bartholomew Fair: monkeys and apes dancing, an Italian girl performing dexterities on the high rope, and her father holding a four-hundred-pound iron by the hairs of his head only. In 1668, when Pepys attended Southwark Fair, on 21 September, he saw a puppet show, *Whittington*, and Jacob Hall's dancing on the ropes, the latter also a Bartholomew Fair specialty.

As at Bartholomew Fair, Southwark Fair had some exhibitions and entertainments which cannot be precisely dated. Miss Rosenfeld has described two: *The Exile of the Earl of Huntington*, given at the Queen's Arms Tavern, and *A New Wonder: A Woman Never Vex'd*, presented at Parker's Booth near the King's Bench. Both were probably performed before the death of Queen Mary in 1694.[73]

MAY FAIR. This Fair developed in the late seventeenth century, a charter being granted in 1688 by James II. By 1696 drolls and interludes had been presented there, and presumably the Fair continued, perhaps flourished, during the remaining years of the century. Little, however, is specifically known of drolls or interludes until 1699, when Ned Ward, visiting the Fair, described its activities. On the whole, May Fair during the last decade of the century had less importance as a place offering dramatic or pseudo-dramatic entertainments than either of ther others.[74]

THE INNS OF COURT

During most of the forty years between 1660 and 1700 two of the Temple Courts—the Inner Temple and the Middle Temple—offered plays, usually two yearly, as part of their festivities. These occurred on All Hallows and Candlemas (1 November and 2 February) or the day following when these fell on Sunday. Ordinarily the Temples invited justices and other dignitaries to a dinner and entertainments, including a play. For the latter the Temples

73 *Ibid.*, p. 75. For a reproduction of one bill, see opposite page 76.
74 For a brief account of May Fair, 1690–1700, see Rosenfeld, *The Theatre of the London Fairs*, pp. 108–9.

usually engaged the Duke's or King's Company to present one from the repertories in the dining hall. The Temples sponsored these entertainments quite regularly during the twenty years following the return of Charles II, but the union of the companies and the troubled times of the 1680's resulted in more sporadic performances, and although the practice continued to the end of the century (and later), the Temples less regularly offered plays at their festivities.

For these performances the companies usually received a fee of £20, and as they ordinarily acted also at the playhouse on the same day, performances at the Temples provided a windfall. As a rule, the Temples chose the more popular dramas, often those from pre-Commonwealth times, such as *The Spanish Curate* or *Rule a Wife and Have a Wife*; but occasionally they chose a contemporary play, such as *The Adventures of Five Hours* or *Love for Love*.

CONCERT HALLS

During the years from 1660 to 1672 the principal musical activities in London were incidental music in the theatres, concerts in private homes and at Court, and musical entertainments presented before the King. Some of these, particularly those by performers who have a relationship to the theatres, are listed in the Calendar. In 1672, however, public concerts, usually involving an admission fee, developed. According to Roger North, John Bannister, the composer, initiated concerts catering to the public at large. The first known advertisement of his offerings appeared in the *London Gazette*, No. 742, 26–30 December 1672: "These are to give notice, that at Mr John Banisters House, (now called the Musick-School) over against the George Tavern in White Fryers, this present Monday, will be Musick performed by excellent Masters, beginning precisely at 4 of the clock in the afternoon, and every afternoon for the future, precisely at the same hour."[75]

Bannister clearly envisioned a comprehensive series of concerts, and although he did not advertise daily, he may have kept his programs with some regularity through the winter of 1672–73. Roger North mentions also another set of concerts, conducted by Ben Wellington, private at first, then public, near St. Gregory's Church, not far from St. Paul's Cathedral. According to North, Bannister's room had tables, seats, and a side box with curtains for the musicians, with a charge of a shilling, whereas Wellington played a

75 See also *Roger North on Music*, ed. John Wilson (London, 1959), pp. 302–3.

chamber organ while "folks heard musick out of the Catch-book, and drank ale together."[76]

A lack of information leaves us in doubt as to the attendance at the first series of musicals, but the persistence of Bannister and the imitation of his programs by other composer-musicians suggest that the public concert caught on rather quickly. Certainly in the last two decades of the century the popularity of the concert hall must have exceeded the expectations of Bannister, for in later seasons the concert halls rivalled the theatres by importing performers from the Continent, by offering prologues and epilogues, by advertising benefits, and by having special concerts in honor of visiting royalty. The concert developed its own accommodations. York Buildings, for example, became a center for the musical arts, and other locations, such as Stationers' Hall, the Two Golden Balls, and Bedford Gate, catered to the enlarging circle of the musically minded. Similarly, just as the theatres presented a great many songs especially composed for plays and entr'acte entertainments, the halls offered a good many songs and instrumental compositions which apparently were expressly created for them. As we know of many songs which were performed in the concert halls for which no specific date has been determined, the listing of concerts in the Calendar is, obviously, not a complete one.

[76] *Ibid.*, pp. 303–4.

Theatrical Financing

NEW CONSTRUCTION

AT THE RESUMPTION of acting in 1660, the new companies naturally sought the best quarters for their operations. Had relatively new and capacious theatres been available, probably the urge to construct additional ones would have been less strong. But the necessity of using the Red Bull, Salisbury Court, the Cockpit in Drury Lane, old structures which had deteriorated, and the converted Gibbons' Tennis Court and Lisle's Tennis Court, failed to provide the managements with fully satisfactory playhouses. As a result, both patent companies bestirred themselves to find financial aid for constructing new ones, particularly those in Dorset Garden and in Bridges Street, Drury Lane.

Sir William Davenant had secured for the Duke's Company Lisle's Tennis Court, which he had sufficiently adapted to the use of changeable scenery and which proved temporarily satisfactory. The King's Company, u.der the direction of Thomas Killigrew, was the first seriously to plan a wholly new playhouse, the Theatre Royal in Bridges Street, Drury Lane. By December 1661 Killigrew had made preparations to construct it at a cost of £1,500 on ground leased from the Earl of Bedford at an annual rent of £50. To finance the construction, the King's Company devised two coordinate enterprises. One was a sharing company, composed of Killigrew and the principal actors. Acting shares totalled 12¾, of which Killigrew had two; two more were unassigned, and the remaining 8¾ were divided, not equally, among eight actors. This arrangement provided for the normal operations of the producing company, the sharers to participate in the profits.[77]

The construction of a new theatre, however, involved the acting company and a number of individuals outside. Essentially three parties were involved: the Earl of Bedford, owner of the site; the acting company (Killigrew and the eight actors); and William Hewett and Robert Clayton, acting as trustees. The first step toward construction was to establish a building

[77] Hotson, *Commonwealth and Restoration Stage*, pp. 243–44.

fund derived from the sale of 36 shares. These were allocated, on 28 January 1661/2, to Sir Robert Howard, Killigrew, and the eight actors in an unequal distribution: nine each to Howard and Killigrew, four to John Lacy (an actor), and two each to the seven other players forming the original acting company of eight sharers. On the same day the acting company (the eight sharers in the building enterprise and five others) agreed to act in the proposed theatre and to pay the building sharers £3 10s. for each acting day. This mode of organizing the finances and charges of a company on the basis of the acting day endured for the next 150 years.[78]

Although the cost of the theatre in Drury Lane had been estimated at £1,500, the actual expenditures rose to approximately £2,400. Presumably, then, each of the 36 shares allocated among the building-sharers involved an investment of £66 13s. 4d.[79] Hotson points out, however, that not long after the opening of the theatre on 7 May 1663, a share sold at the rate of £215, indicating a strong confidence in the prosperity of the company and success in this mode of financing.

The next building enterprise was the construction of Dorset Garden Theatre, envisioned by Sir William Davenant and completed after his death. In anticipation of its financing, Davenant devised a system somewhat different from that employed by Killigrew. Before planning the house, Davenant arranged to hold for himself ten out of fifteen shares in the acting company (Duke's).[80] Instead, then, of forming a second set of sharers, as had been done to finance Drury Lane, Davenant alone sold seven and seven-tenths of his shares to secure building capital. He disposed of his units at prices ranging from £600 to £800.[81]

By 1670 the Duke's Company was ready to build. It leased a site in Dorset Garden for a period of 39 years at an annual rent of £130, considerably more than the sum charged for the leased land on which Drury Lane was constructed. In mid-1670 the sharers[82] agreed to raise among themselves £3,000 to finance the theatre, each contributing in proportion to his share and binding himself to contribute more if this sum was insufficient,[83] as indeed it turned out to be. To repay the sharers, sufficient income was set aside on each acting day to amortize within four years their original contributions, less each sharer's part of the ground rent and taxes.

[78] *Ibid.*
[79] *Ibid.*, p. 249.
[80] *Ibid.*, p. 207.
[81] *Ibid.*, pp. 219–21.
[82] *Ibid.*, p. 230. By this time, by complicated arrangements, the number of shares had been increased from fifteen to twenty.
[83] *Ibid.*, p. 229.

Even though the estimated cost of Dorset Garden was more than the actual cost of the first Drury Lane, the sum of £3,000 proposed for it proved inadequate. Hotson has estimated that the actual expenditures rose to £9,000, three times the initial estimate, the increase being borne by further payments from the sharers.[84]

The third and the last wholly new theatre constructed in the seventeenth century was the second Drury Lane, erected after the first one was destroyed by fire in January 1672. The ruined one had cost £2,400, and as the building investors had received £3 10s. each acting day (as contrasted with £7 later at Dorset Gardens), negotiations for the rebuilding were predicated upon the figures for the first one. It was agreed, however, that the sum of £3 10s. each acting day was to be paid on each share to the building investors *if* the cost came to £2,400, proportionally more if the costs rose.[85] Although an exact figure seems not to have been recorded in contemporary documents, Hotson, by comparing the proposed payment of £3 10s. with the actual one, £5 14s., estimates the ultimate cost as approximately £3,900. In addition, the company financed the building of a new scene-house, the purchase of scenes and costumes to replace those lost in the fire, by additional contributions from each sharer, to a total of £2,040. No contemporary statement indicates whether the first Drury Lane was covered by insurance or in what way, if at all, the original building investors received compensation for that loss, other than previous payments.[86]

The last seventeenth-century venture in theatrical building was a conversion for Betterton and his associates, as noted above, not the erection of a new structure. Although Betterton and company had the support of influential courtiers, they lacked great resources in their private holdings. In converting the Tennis Court in Lincoln's Inn Fields, the sharing actors obtained a voluntary subscription of twenty to forty guineas from an undesignated number of sponsors.[87] Cibber's report of these events suggests that the subscriptions were gifts, not loans. As a result, we have little genuine information concerning the financial resources of this company or the extent to which it received a sum sufficient to outfit the theatre with scenes, properties, and costumes. Although the company had a very satisfactory opening season (1694–95), it had by the season of 1696–97 run into financial

[84] *Ibid.*, p. 232.

[85] *Ibid.*, p. 254.

[86] As the Sun Insurance Office, Ltd., of London, which shared in the insuring of the later Drury Lane playhouses, was not founded until 1710, it has no records of earlier arrangements concerning fire insurance on the seventeenth-century properties.

[87] Cibber, *Apology*, I, 194.

difficulties. The details are vague, but a petition by John Verbruggen indicates that the Betterton-Barry-Bracegirdle management was in debt. Verbruggen heard once (apparently in the season of 1696–97) that the deficit was less than £200 but later that it amounted to £800.[88] Probably some of this indebtedness resulted from the expense of converting and supplying the theatre under the handicap of shortness of time as well as money and under competition from a company better equipped with the technical requirements of a producing company—except fine actors.

FINANCIAL OPERATIONS

Relatively little is known of the daily financial operations of the Restoration theatres, for, unfortunately, no account books survive for this period, only isolated and fragmentary data. Hence, it is impossible to reconstruct the probable income and expenditures for all types of theatrical operations. At best, one can exemplify the types of income and suggest the range of basic costs and kinds of disbursements.

INCOME. Because the only major source of income for the playhouse was the box-office receipts, prudence dictated that basic financial arrangements be predicated upon daily receipts. If the theatres were closed, as they were during part of Lent and the summer, Christmas holidays, and for at least six weeks on the death of royalty of the highest rank, the companies could not afford to obligate themselves to payments (except for taxes and rents) unless the disbursements were contingent upon the daily income from acting. The long closure of the playhouses during the Great Plague would have bankrupted the companies had their obligations for salaries and wages rested on an annual instead of an "acting day" basis.[89]

The scarcity of documents makes it difficult to discover precisely the income of the theatres either day-by-day or according to categories. Nevertheless, summaries of some financial records suggest the nature of the income.

88 Nicoll, *Restoration Drama*, pp. 384–85.

89 As an illustration of the practical relationships of receipts and charges, let us take the United Company in the early 1690's when Christopher Rich, a principal proprietor, was obligated to pay £3 each acting day at the Theatre Royal or £7 each acting day at Dorset Garden. Had he been obliged to pay an annual rate, whether the theatres were open or not, the results financially would have been disastrous. On the other hand, he was free to choose where to stage a particular drama; if a spectacle might bring higher receipts in the larger theatre, he could afford to offer it in Dorset Garden and pay the higher charge. For a play likely to attract a smaller, more intimate audience, with lower receipts, he might well produce it at Drury Lane.

For example, as a result of litigation, we know that from 4 May 1682 to 3 August 1692 the United Company received £103,988 5s. 7d. As this period covered, roughly, ten seasons, the receipts, as Hotson indicates,[90] averaged £10,400 a year, approximately £50 daily for an acting season of two hundred performances. This was a profitable level of operations, but not a superlatively high average. Too few examples of daily or yearly receipts exist for the period from 1660 to 1700 to warrant detailed comparisons between the income of the United Company from 1682 to 1692 and that for any other period. Nevertheless, statements by Pepys and Downes suggest that between 1660 and 1670 (except for the Plague) both the Duke's and King's Company experienced good returns. Downes estimated that the Duke's Company took in £1,000 from Etherege's *The Comical Revenge* during its first month, and Evelyn reported, perhaps erroneously, that Tuke's *The Adventures of Five Hours* might be worth £4,000 to £5,000 to the players.

The extremes in daily receipts may be more concretely illustrated. Downes reported that Shadwell received £130 for his benefit at *The Squire of Alsatia*, more than any one else received at Drury Lane for a play at ordinary admission charges.[91] A very popular play might well bring as much as £100 nightly on the best days of its run. On the other hand, during the spring of 1681 the receipts on at least nineteen days fell below the level of basic charges, dipping on 11 May 1681, for example, to £3 14s. 6d.[92] Sometimes it was more profitable to dismiss than to play and incur the customary charges for an acting day.

Supplementing the regular receipts, a small but fairly regular source of income known as After-Money appeared. It was a device initiated for receiving lesser sums (usually one half the ordinary charge) for admittance after the third act, hence the name. The diaries of Samuel Pepys and James Brydges and orders forbidding the practice make it evident that many spectators came late, sometimes to see an act or two, bobbing in and out of the theatres at their leisure. If the spectator could be forced or persuaded to pay for the privilege of seeing a portion of the play, the theatres stood to gain financially from this distracting habit. Actually, the sums realized were of substantial benefit to the treasurer. In a petition of the players, December 1694, After-Money reportedly brought in £700 or £800 yearly, an average of £3 10s. to £4 nightly in a season of two hundred acting days. In the light

90 *Commonwealth and Restoration Stage*, pp. 288–89.
91 *Roscius Anglicanus*, p. 41. It should be remembered that on a benefit night the treasurer of the company did not retain for the use of the playhouse the entire sum; the dramatist was entitled to the difference between the total receipts and the house charges.
92 Hotson, *Commonwealth and Restoration Stage*, p. 267.

of an average yearly income of £10,400 for the United Company, After-Money provided an additional 7 or 8 per cent of revenue.93

Concessions, such as the privilege of selling fruit in the theatres, provided another minor but steady source of income. The best known of the fruiterers was Mary Meggs, familiarly called Orange Moll, who secured a license from the King's Company, 10 February 1662/3, to sell oranges, lemons, other fruits and sweetmeats, in the new Drury Lane, for which she paid £100, plus 6s. 8d. each acting day. During a season of two hundred performances, the daily payment would add approximately £66 to the resources of the company. After her death this concession was assigned to Thomas Phillips, 21 August 1695, for seven years at a payment of 13s. 4d. each acting day, a doubling of the previous amount.94 During an ordinary season this concession should have added at least £132 to the company's accounts.

Additional minor sources of net income came from within the companies, but these can hardly have provided appreciable financial gain to a properly functioning group. One such source was the forfeit. According to the Patentees, replying to allegations, all forfeits were put into the general receipts.95 The amounts charged for violations of articles were stated in a proposed set for a company under date of 9 December 1675: For disposing of roles without the consent of the company, 20s. For refusal of a part, a week's salary. For neglect of rehearsal, the sum not indicated. For taking properties, without permission, from the playhouse, a week's salary.96 As was true of other types of forfeits, these might bring a slightly higher net income, but they would not materially alter the financial circumstances of a company.

DISBURSEMENTS.   Just as a scarcity of documents makes it difficult to be precise concerning the daily income, so it is impossible to present in detail the varied expenditures of the producing companies. One of the prevailing fixed expenses was the payment to the building investors, due on each acting day, which was intended not only to liquidate the investment in the construction of the theatre but also to provide a profitable return upon the capital. As previously indicated, this cost was, for Dorset Garden, £5 for the first year after its construction, then £6 for two years, then £7.97

93 In an affidavit, Alexander Davenant claimed the distinction of having discovered that useful income could be secured by the device of After Money. See Hotson, *Commonwealth and Restoration Stage*, p. 290.

94 *Ibid.*, p. 310.

95 This statement was made in 1694. See Nicoll, *Restoration Drama*, p. 374.

96 *Ibid.*, p. 324 n.

97 Hotson, *Commonwealth and Restoration Stage*, p. 232.

Other constant charges for which we do not know the details concern the printing and posting of bills to announce each day's performance, candles,[98] payments for costumes, scenes, and machines. Although orders for habits and properties exist, they are so sporadic that yearly estimates would be meaningless.[99] Sometimes costs ran very high. For example, the clothes, scenes, and music for *The Fairy Queen* (2 May 1692) apparently came to £3,000.[100]

The major basic outlay, however, was for salaries and wages. When the greater actors were sharers and the theatre was prosperous, their income was derived from the profits; but they had to pay a large corps of hirelings and a multitude of behind-the-scenes personnel. In a report upon his duties, Thomas Cross, a treasurer, referred to salaries for hirelings, music masters, dancing masters, scene men, barbers, wardrobe-keepers, doorkeepers, soldiers (guards), and he might well have mentioned prompter, bookkeeper, treasurers, tiring men and women. In addition, he referred to the payment of bills for "Scenes, Habits, Properties, Candles, Oil, and other things."[101]

Occasionally we get glimpses into actual costs. The receipts for two performances at Drury Lane on 12 and 26 December 1677 record that the sum set aside for the shareholders came to £5 14s. nightly.[102] At one time John Rogers received a grant of one shilling in every twenty received in each playhouse for himself and assistants as guards for all the public theatres,[103] but how long this exorbitant rate continued is not known. Furthermore, in the last decade of the century some records exist of the range of salaries to actors. Around 1694 Mrs Barry received 50s. weekly; Betterton, discontinuing a sharing agreement, £5 weekly and a yearly present of fifty guineas; Williams, £4 weekly; and proposed articles for Bullock and Sorin called for 20s. and 30s. weekly, respectively.[104] These isolated figures, however, do not suggest the total weekly payroll.

A more exact indication of costs appears in the figure known as the Daily Charge, a summation of all expenses averaged out to show the point between profit and loss. For the opening decades of the Restoration this figure is not known, but in the season of 1694–95 the Patentees, on 17 De-

---

98 See Thomas Killigrew's remarks to Pepys, 12 February 1666/7 concerning his use of wax candles, more expensive than the outmoded tallow ones.

99 A number of these are in Nicoll, *Restoration Drama*, and in Alwin Thaler, *Shakespere to Sheridan* (Cambridge, Mass., 1922).

100 Luttrell, *A Brief Relation*, II, 435.

101 Hotson, *Commonwealth and Restoration Stage*, p. 222.

102 Fitzgerald, *A New History*, I, 145.

103 British Museum Egerton MS. 2537, Nicholas Papers, V. fol. 275.

104 Nicoll, *Restoration Drama*, pp. 269, 370, 384.

cember 1694, asserted that the full expense of the United Company amounted to £30 each acting day;[105] by the season of 1699–1700 the charge had risen to £34.[106] Probably the basic daily expense of the theatres rose gradually from 1660 to 1700, perhaps from £25 at the Restoration to nearly £35 at the close of the century. The inflationary aspect of increases in salaries and costs of new scenery and machinery contributed to a steady rise.

PROFITS. Without account books, no specific figures for the profits and losses season-by-season exist. Nevertheless, some general conclusions concerning the course of theatrical prosperity can be made. During the period from 1660 to 1670 the novelty of theatrical presentations, the large number of successful new and revived plays, and the enthusiasm of the companies apparently created a congenial atmosphere for playgoing, except during the long darkness of the Great Plague. Hotson points out that by 1663 a share in the King's Theatre had in three years increased in value by 300 per cent.[107] During this period, except for the duration of the Plague, both companies seem to have done well financially until the high costs of the construction of the Dorset Garden Theatre and the destruction by fire of the Theatre Royal in Drury Lane weakened the financial position of both houses. From that time to 1682 the status of the King's Company clearly declined, as indicated by dwindling attendance and internal dissension; its profits apparently dropped markedly. (As already indicated, its receipts on several days in 1681 fell disastrously below the costs of operation.) During the regime of the United Company the combined operations showed a moderate profit, as already indicated by the average receipts of £50 daily when the corresponding house charges were probably not much greater than £30.[108] In the season of 1694–95 the dissatisfaction of Betterton, Mrs Barry, Mrs Bracegirdle and others ended the Union and initiated a period of variable prosperity. From 1695 to the end of the century the Patentees at Drury Lane and Dorset Garden were less prosperous than the new company at Lincoln's Inn Fields, which had the support of many influential literary persons and courtiers. In the last two seasons of the century both companies seem to have drawn closer together in financial stability, a position they kept into the early years of the next century.

[105] *Ibid.*, p. 375.
[106] *A Comparison Between the Two Stages*, p. 8.
[107] *Commonwealth and Restoration Stages*, p. 249.
[108] *Ibid.*, p. 283.

Management and Operations

COMPANY ORGANIZATION

AFTER the structure of the patent companies had settled into the patterns achieved in 1660 and 1661, both—the King's under Thomas Killigrew and the Duke's under Sir William Davenant—had fundamentally the same organizational plan. At the head was the proprietor, who had achieved his position principally by his ability to secure a patent and permission to assemble a group of actors and a stock of plays. In awarding a two-company monopoly to Davenant and Killigrew, the King determined in actuality for many seasons and in principle for many decades this type of organization as a dominant one in the London theatres.

Fortunately, both proprietors were experienced men of the theatre, Davenant possessing the greater technical competence, and both had well-defined ideas concerning the proper conduct of a company and the nature of a successful repertory. Each assembled a company, recruiting, first of all, individuals who had theatrical experience before or during the Commonwealth. As the long dramatic interregnum had limited the number of trained actors, the companies had at first a small number of the traditional boy actors to play female roles as well as a few men with genuine theatrical experience. Almost immediately the proprietors introduced women onto the stage and revolutionized the acting of female roles. In addition, the companies had the good fortune to find quickly young men as talented as Thomas Betterton and Henry Harris.

To effect an organization, the companies, as noted above, created a group of sharing actors and a second category—the hirelings—who might eventually become sharers. Sir William Davenant's agreement (5 November 1660) specifies how the proprietor and players intended to organize themselves. Until Davenant could move into a new theatre, the net profits of the company were to be allocated to fourteen shares, with Davenant, as master and proprietor, possessing four. Thomas Betterton, a young, promising actor, was to be one of his deputies to oversee the accounts.[109] When Davenant

---

[109] *Ibid.*, p. 207. See also Herbert, *Dramatic Records*, pp. 96–100.

and his company moved into a new theatre, the arrangements were more elaborately spelled out, but the principles were essentially the same. Of the (now) fifteen shares, two were assigned to Davenant to cover the rentals, building, and scene frames, and an additional one for the supplying of costumes, properties, and scenes. Of the remaining twelve shares, Davenant kept seven for maintaining the actresses, and five were allotted to the sharing actors. As master, Davenant was to provide three receivers or treasurers. Two or three members of the company were to control the general operations, but Davenant was to appoint the wardrobe keeper, the barber, and half of the doorkeepers, all of these to be paid out of gross receipts. In spelling out the arrangements, it was agreed that, although Davenant received shares in return for his providing costumes and habits, he was not to pay for hats, feathers, gloves, and shoes out of this fund.[110]

Although the details are lacking, Killigrew and the King's Company probably had similar arrangements. Some light is thrown upon the problems of the proprietor in relation to sharing and nonsharing actors through disagreements between Killigrew and his players developing by 1663, as a result of which he delegated the practical direction of plays and rehearsals to Michael Mohun, Charles Hart, and John Lacy. When this new arrangement did not succeed, Killigrew withdrew the delegated power and restored portions of shares to the company from actors who had previously relinquished theirs to become hirelings. In this disagreement the Lord Chamberlain generally supported Killigrew on the grounds of the broad powers granted to him in his patent.[111]

The formal structure, then, of this type of arrangement consisted of a proprietor (the largest shareholder), who was the master of the company in both theatrical and financial affairs; a small number of sharing actors,[112] who received a proportion of the profits after the gross receipts had provided for the major expenses; and a larger number of actors on salary. To these should be added the nonacting personnel: musicians, scenekeepers, tiring men and women, barber, bookkeeper, prompter, machinists, treasurers, and,

[110] Hotson, *Commonwealth and Restoration Stage*, p. 207; Herbert, *Dramatic Records*, pp. 96–100.

[111] Hotson, *Commonwealth and Restoration Stage*, pp. 244–45.

[112] An example of the early arrangements is the Davenant agreement of 5 November 1660: Davenant, as proprietor; Thomas Betterton, Thomas Sheppey, Robert Nokes, James Nokes, Thomas Lovell, John Moseley, Cave Underhill, Robert Turner, and Thomas Lilleston, as actor-sharers; and Henry Harris, also an actor, as a third party. To this list would be added the hirelings. See Hotson, *Commonwealth and Restoration Stage*, p. 206. The relation of this group to the company at large can be seen in the list of members of the King's Company in the autumn of 1663: 15 actors and 8 actresses. (See E. S. de Beer, *Bulletin of the Institute of Historical Research*, XIX [1942–43], 24.)

in later years, specialists in singing and dancing. In addition, Killigrew, in a confidential moment on 24 January 1668/9, told Pepys that he had on his payroll, at twenty shillings weekly, a woman to serve the sexual comfort of eight or ten of the young men of the house, "whom till he did so he could never keep to their business, and now he do." This mode of organization persisted in both companies until the death of Davenant in 1668; the proprietorship then became a problem for the Davenant family, at whose request Thomas Betterton and Henry Harris governed as masters under Lady Davenant. Although this arrangement had its tensions, the Duke's Company sufficiently prospered to be the dominant one by the time (1682) the ailing King's Company was absorbed into the United Company.

After 1670 the King's Company formulated rules and principles which reflected its operating problems. One major difficulty which the companies and the Lord Chamberlain struggled with for decades concerned control over actors who wished to change from one group to another. At this time, the King's Company insisted that no one should quit his position without three months' notice. (Later, as we shall see, this rule became more stringent.) A corollary principle was a requirement that no man or woman should dispose of parts without the consent of the company; furthermore, no player was to refuse a part if the company thought him suited to it. As for beginners, the management attempted to regulate their induction by insisting that no one should be entered on the rolls without the full consent of the members and that apprentices should serve three probationary months without pay. The other regulations dealt chiefly with problems of decorum and propriety. The organgewoman and her assistants in selling fruit, being very noisy, should behave more decorously. There were to be no disorders at the sharing table, and no one should interfere with proceedings in the tiring room. No feathers, clothes, or ribbons were to be taken away without the consent of the company, and no costumes were to be removed from the playhouse. (Because individuals often supplied their own gloves, shoes, and ornaments, the management had to make distinctions between personal and company property.) Essentially, these principles were a codification of practices which required regulation and definition.[113]

With the union of the companies in 1682, some of these regulations fell into desuetude. With but one London company, an actor had little choice of contract. If he was unhappy in his position, he might tour the provinces (a risky proposition) or go to Edinburgh or Dublin (somewhat more appealing), but remaining in London meant accepting the terms of

[113] Nicoll, *Restoration Drama*, pp. 324n, 325n.

the single company. During the union the proprietorship devolved principally upon members of the Davenant family, as Thomas Killigrew lost his
controlling position, but the Davenant family, with some exceptions, had the
necessary theatrical experience with which to operate a company successfully.

In the 1690's, however, a reorganization of management occurred.
With the dissolution of the Davenant regime, control of the United Company
passed into the hands of Christopher Rich, a man with no experience in the
theatre either as actor, playwright, or manager, and Sir Thomas Skipwith,
who was equally insensitive to the nature of a proper theatrical enterprise.
Then, really for the first time since the Restoration, the company came
under the direction of proprietors whose only real interest in the enterprise
was its financial success. Other considerations—the quality of acting, the
harmony of the players, the nature of the daily program, and the plays—were
of importance only if they contributed to the financial betterment of the
proprietors. Inevitably this form of management brought dissension, especially among the talented and experienced actors. In 1695 matters came to
a crisis, and during the closing of the theatres after the death of Queen
Mary, a seceding group gained the permission and support of the government
to start a new company. The principals were Thomas Betterton, Elizabeth
Barry, and Anne Bracegirdle, three of the most talented players in the United
Company. The sharing company they formed centered for the first time
formal control in a small number of sharing actors without a proprietor. In
principle, the members professed equality of shares, for it was agreed, at
least tentatively, that not more than ten sharers would be permitted and
that no one was to have more than a single share.[114]

With the re-establishment of two companies, each reflecting a different
theory of management, some of the old problems reappeared. Arbitrary
decisions by the Rich-Skipwith regime caused an occasional player to desire
a transfer to the sharing group under Betterton. On the other hand, his
company discovered that some members did not relish rule by their equals,
for at one time Thomas Dogget, dissatisfied with the Betterton organization
desired leave to join the rival company. The request posed a problem for
the Lord Chamberlain, who had ruled that individuals could leave one
company for another only with full consent of all concerned. A compromise
was effected when John Verbruggen, weary of the Rich-Skipwith management at the same time that Dogget wished to join it, became part of an
exchange. The Lord Chamberlain, however, stated clearly that this was
not to happen again.

[114] *Ibid.*, pp. 361–62.

During the forty years from 1660 to 1700 few writers discussed the theory and practice of management, but Colley Cibber, who joined the United Company in 1690, felt that his experiences with the Rich-Skipwith management had taught him one lesson: "My having been a Witness of this unnecessary Rupture [the secession in the season of 1694–95] was of great use to me when, many Years after, I came to be a Menager my self. I laid it down as a settled Maxim, that no Company could flourish while the chief Actors and the Undertakers were at variance." As a specific example of mismanagement, he pointed out that the Patentees, to reduce salaries, gave Betterton's roles and Mrs Barry's chief parts to George Powell and Anne Bracegirdle. Powell accepted this arrangement, with resulting hard feeling, but Mrs Bracegirdle had the perception to know that this procedure would not work out well and she refused the offer.[115] With a different perspective, John Dennis, possibly disgruntled by the treatment of his plays by managers, some years later compared the management of 1660 with that of the last decade:

> The theater was not then [immediately following the Restoration] as it is now in Hands of Players, illiterate, unthinking, unjust, ungratefull and sordid. . . . At The Restoration the Theaters were in the Hands of Gentlemen, who had Done particular services to the Crown, and who were peculiarly qualifyd for the Discharge of that Important Trust. They had Honour, learning, breeding, Discernment, Integrity, Impartiality and generosity. Their chief aim was to see that the Town was well entertaind and The Drama improvd. They alterd all at once the whole Face of the Stage by introducing scenes and women; which added probability to the Dramatick Actions and made every thing look more naturally. When any new Dramatick performance was brought them, They never asked who had seen it, who had recommended it, or what Numbers were to support it, They knew that if it had merit it would support it self, and of its merit, They were very well able to Judge. By these methods men of the finest parts were animated to write for the stage, and noe one was Discourgd by His obscurity or because He had not appeard before. And twas for this Reason that more good Comedies were writt from 1660 to 1700, During all which time The Theater was in the Hands of Gentlemen, than will be writt in a Thousand years if the Management lies in the Players.[116]

Although Dennis uses dates rather loosely, he appears to be referring primarily to the period before 1690, after which the stage fell into the hands of nongentlemen. In addition, his strictures upon actor-managers probably

---

[115] *Apology*, I, 188–90.
[116] *The Causes of the Decay and Defects of Dramatick Poetry* (ca. 1725) in Dennis, *Works*, ed. E. N. Hooker (Baltimore, 1943), II, 277–78.

refer primarily to the Cibber-Wilks-Booth management of the early eighteenth century than to the Betterton-Barry-Bracegirdle triumvirate of the last decade of the seventeenth century.

LICENSING, THE LORD CHAMBERLAIN, AND THE MASTER OF THE REVELS

The practical and formal relationships between management and governmental officials who possessed, or sought to increase, control over the content as well as propriety of plays posed serious problems for management. At the establishment of the two patent companies in 1660, the new patentees, Davenant and Killigrew, came into conflict with Sir Henry Herbert, who, holding the long-established sinecure of Master of the Revels, wished to retain and extend the power of his office over all plays, theatres, actors, and companies. When the patentees negotiated with Charles II for their licenses, Herbert protested vigorously and attempted, by an appeal to precedent, to establish the authority of the Master of the Revels above that of the patentees. After Sir Henry had been sworn into office, 20 June 1660, he attempted to increase his revenue by having a group of actors pay his office a fee of 40s. for each new play and 20s. for each revived one. For the next two years he waged constant battle to establish his prerogatives. On 6 May 1662 he issued a statement clarifying and establishing the status of his office with respect to the patent companies. By 4 June 1662 he had come to an agreement with Killigrew's Company, and on 11 July 1662 he restated his claim to the fees due to him for new and revised plays.[117]

Nevertheless, it is uncertain how potent a challenge the Master of the Revels continued to be. Although one set of accounts for 1663 and 1664 shows payments of £41 "For Playes" to Herbert, the lack of similar records for later years leaves unsettled the regularity of such payments. After Herbert left the office, it may have lost some of its power, but during the 1680's, when the Popish Plot inflamed London, and the 1690's, when fresh anti-stage sentiment appeared, the Master of the Revels and the Lord Chamberlain clearly turned their attention to political and licentious elements. Certainly the two offices possessed decisive powers to censor and prohibit plays, especially for political reasons, and this censorship struck the theatres most acutely during the tension of the Popish Plot (1679–82), during the short reign of James II, and during the transition to the rule of William and Mary.

[117] See Herbert, *Dramatic Records*, pp. 108–23, 138.

At the time of the Popish Plot, *Lucius Junius Brutus* was acted three days, then silenced on 11 December 1680. Contemporaneously, Nahum Tate's *Sicilian Usurper* (an adaptation of *Richard II*) was forbidden at Drury Lane on 14 December 1680, and when the theatre revived it a month later under a variant title, the authorities silenced the playhouse for ten days. John Crowne's *The City Politiques* was forbidden on 26 June 1682. On 18 July of the same year *The Duke of Guise* suffered banishment but was later allowed to appear (28 November 1682), when the atmosphere was quieter. According to the Epilogue, *The Massacre of Paris*, 7 November 1689, had once been suppressed, apparently at the request of the French Ambassador. In the final decade of the century Dryden's *Cleomenes* was forbidden (9 April 1692) on political grounds, but the authorities lifted the ban by 16 April 1692.

In addition to outright banishment (often reversed), plays suffered partial restrictions. In the Preface to *The Lancashire Witches* (September 1681), Shadwell pointed out that the Master of the Revels at first licensed the play "with little alteration," but, after complaints, he reviewed the play and expunged considerable portions. This case is one piece of evidence supporting the likelihood that new plays had to be approved by the Revels. A year or so later the Lord Chamberlain held up Crowne's *The City Politiques* for a considerable period because of its political implications, but this seems to be an example of censorship of the play as a whole rather than alteration of parts of it, as was the case with *The Lancashire Witches*.[118] At the end of the century further evidence points to continued examination of new plays by the Master of the Revels or the Lord Chamberlain. On 4 June 1694 the Lord Chamberlain issued an order directing that all new dramas must be brought to his office for scrutiny.[119] The effects of this order appear in an advertisement of *The World in the Moon* in the *Post Boy*, 29 June–1 July 1697, which states: "It is licensed by the Lord Chamberlain's Secretary, and the Master of the Revels," and in the treatment of Cibber's *Richard III*, ca. December 1699, when, in Cibber's report, the Master of the Revels "expung'd the whole first Act, without sparing a Line of it."[120]

Coincident with the problem of political censorship an anti-stage sentiment emerged with the Restoration loosening of the moral reins which the Commonwealth had held tightly. With the arrival of Charles II in England, actions, none very successful, leading toward suppression of the

[118] See the Calendar, 19 January 1682/3.
[119] L. C. 5/152, in J. W. Krutch, *Comedy and Conscience after the Restoration*, rev. ed. (New York, 1949), p. 181. This order may simply be a reiteration of earlier ones, the new statement growing out of the anti-stage agitation at the end of the century.
[120] *Apology*, I, 275.

players were initiated. On 23 April 1660 General Monk and the Council of State issued an order against plays, warning all theatres to desist at their peril.[121] On 20 August 1660, when the patent companies undertook to make their position secure, Davenant drafted a warrant (in *Calendar of State Papers Domestic*)[122] which he hoped to have used against the companies at the Red Bull, the Cockpit in Drury Lane, and Salisbury Court. Although the warrant was intended for this purpose, Davenant used as a part of his argument the suppression of plays and entertainments which tend to "prophaneness, scurrility, obsceneness, and other abuses."

Linked with these movements was a continued public effort to suppress all profaneness and licentiousness. Part of this attitude doubtless constituted lip service to public morality, but the incessant attention paid to it by the authorities had a nagging effect upon the playhouses. The regulations began as early as 13 October 1660, when Sir Henry Herbert sent a warrant to Michael Mohun, at the Cockpit, Drury Lane, advising his troupe to submit all intended plays for reformation of all profaneness and ribaldry. Nevertheless, only an occasional play seems to have banned for its general effect (other than political grounds), such as the banning by Charles II on 22 March 1662/3 of John Wilson's *The Cheats*, which had been certified for presentation only two weeks earlier.

Another factor in public disapproval stemmed from the eagerness of the playhouses to resume acting after the long closure because of the Plague. Pepys, writing on 15 October 1666, referred to outcries at the presentation of plays at Court before the virulence of the Plague had subsided; and the report that the theatres had made contributions to charity in order to secure permission added to the impression that the management placed profit above public welfare. One need only to read John Evelyn's *Diary* to note the deeply ingrained moral disapproval of the stage.

In the closing decade of the century, however, anti-stage sentiment re-established itself more firmly. When Betterton and his associates opened their dissident theatre, some elements in Lincoln's Inn Fields opposed it on the usual grounds of danger to decency and morality.[123] By 1698 the strength of the moral opposition centered in the publications of Jeremy Collier, especially his *A Short View of the Immorality and Prophaneness of the English Stage* (1698), which, coupled with the activities of the Societies for the Reformation of Manners, stimulated a variety of actions against the

121 See *Parliamentary Intelligence*, 30 April 1660, and *Diurnal of Thomas Rugg, 1659–1661*, ed. W. L. Sachse, April 1660. Camden Society, Third Series, XCI (London, 1961).

122 P. 196. See Hotson, *Commonwealth and Restoration Stage*, p. 201.

123 Luttrell, *A Brief Relation*, III, 542.

theatres. On 10 February 1697/8, shortly before Collier's book appeared, the Commons addressed the King on profaneness in general and the play-houses in particular.[124] No doubt, the implications in Collier's book were already in the wind,[125] for in May 1698 the Justices of Middlesex made a presentment against the playhouses as nurseries of debauchery and blasphemy, specifying Congreve's *The Double Dealer* and D'Urfey's *Don Quixote*.[126] So far as the relations between management, on the one hand, and the authorities and segments of the public were concerned, the period from 1690 to 1710 was probably the most critical one for the playhouses, with the possible exception of the years of the Popish Plot, during the late seventeenth and early eighteenth centuries.

MAINTAINING DECORUM

A less serious but nevertheless vexing concern was the maintenance of decorum within the playhouses. Extremely disturbing were the numerous altercations, some of which led to sword play within the theatres and occasionally to duels outside. These not only inconvenienced and endangered the spectators but also destroyed the proper esthetic atmosphere for actors and auditors. It is difficult to know how frequently such engagements occurred, for probably only the most flagrant episodes were reported in letters, diaries, and newspapers, but a systematic reading of the daily Calendar suggests that the quickness of a gentleman's honor to flame under an affront caused minor and major disturbances. A single example reported by Charles Hatton, 2 September 1675, may suffice: "Last Saturday at ye Dukes play-house ther happened a quarrel between Mr Scroppe, who was in drinke, and Sr Tho: Armstronge. Mr Scroope gave Sr Tho: very ill language and, at last, drew upon him: whereupon Sr Tho: drew, and ye first passe ran Mr Scroope through ye heart, who fell dead upon ye place without speaking a word."[127]

On a less tragic level a variety of incidents affected the tone of the theatre. Pepys' brief but graphic account of a man's choking on an orange, 2 November 1667, and his rescue from death by the deft ministrations of Orange Moll (Mary Meggs) is an unforgettable vignette and an example of

---

124 *Ibid.*, IV, 342.
125 For a full list of the works treating the controversial Collier attack, see *The Works of John Dennis*, I, 468–70.
126 Luttrell, *A Brief Relation*, 10 and 12 May 1698, IV, 378–79.
127 *Hatton Correspondence*, Camden Society, 1878, XXII, 121.

e

an interruption prejudicial to proper dramatic atmosphere. On another occasion, 18 February 1666/7, Pepys vividly portrays the distracting influence of conversation among the auditors. On that occasion Pepys thoroughly enjoyed the wit of Sir Charles Sedley's remarks but confessed that he "lost the pleasure of the play wholly." The Epilogue to Lee's *Sophonisba*, no doubt exaggerating, suggests the irritation of those sensing the confusion in the audience:

> One half o' the Play they spend in noise and brawl,
> Sleep out the rest, then wake and damn it all.

The Prologue to *Cleomenes* emphasizes the actors' complaints concerning the wits and fops:

> Who to save Coach-hire, trudge along the Street,
> Then print our Matted Seats with dirty Feet;
> Who, while we speak, make Love to Orange Wenches,
> And between Acts stand strutting on the Benches.

On another occasion, 1 May 1668, Pepys and other spectators had their concentration utterly ruined by rain falling upon them from a cupola in the roof.

Further evidence concerning the problems of maintaining a proper decorum appears in numerous orders, no doubt issued at the request of the management. Frequently the Lord Chamberlain ordered any one not properly entitled to access to the tiring room to refrain from disturbing the players there.[128] Similar directives restricted unauthorized persons from appearing behind the scenes or on stage, lest they interfere with the proper working of the scenes and the progress of the play.[129] Of less importance yet inevitably a cause of complaint was the misbehavior of the musicians who, irritating the gentlemen by wearing their hats in the theatre, were ordered to appear uncovered.[130] The tricks of the orangewomen had a disturbing effect upon the audience; Pepys, on 11 May 1668, though clearly amused by their manners, was irked by their deceptiveness. And management may have been concerned also in the controversy concerning women who wore vizard-masks in the playhouses, for the practice provoked flirtation at the expense of concentration upon the play. As early as 12 June 1663 Pepys refers

---

[128] 25 February 1663/4 and 16 May 1668. See Fitzgerald, *A New History*, I, 96, and *Calendar State Papers Domestic*, 1667-68, pp. 394-95.

[129] See L. C. 7/1, fol. 6, 18 Jan. 1686/7, in Nicoll, *Restoration Drama*, p. 360; *Calendar State Papers Domestic*, 1689-90, pp. 321-22.

[130] L. C. 5/153, in Nicoll, *Restoration Drama*, p. 361.

to this custom. At the end of the century (see 12 May 1698) the Justices of Middlesex thought the custom sufficiently disturbing that they issued a presentment against women frequenting the playhouses in masks.[131]

As a manager, Thomas Killigrew worked hard to improve the accommodations and practices at the King's Theatre. He confided to Pepys (12 February 1666/7) in some detail the conditions which he had brought about:

> That the stage is now by his pains a thousand times better and more glorious than ever heretofore. Now, wax-candles, and many of them; then, not above 3 lbs. of tallow: now, all things civil, no rudeness anywhere; then, as in a bear-garden: then, two or three fiddlers; now, nine or ten of the best; then, nothing but rushes upon the ground, and every thing else mean; and now, all otherwise: then, the Queen seldom and the King never would come; now, not the King only for state, but all civil people do think they may come as well as any.

TIMES OF PERFORMANCE

During the forty years from 1660 to 1700 the days of performing and the acting holidays remained fairly constant. The age developed traditions which the following century observed in principle, though differing in detail. As Count Cominges, visiting in London in 1666, stated: Londoners enjoy a variety of diversions, "the chief one being comedy, which is given every day, Sundays and holidays excepted."[132] This schedule prevailed from October to June, with less frequent acting from June through September.[133]

The companies rigidly observed certain nonacting days. No performances certainly falling on Sunday have been found, and whenever a list

---

[131] Luttrell, A Brief Relation, IV, 379.

[132] J. J. Jusserand, "A French View of England in 1666," Nineteenth Century, LXXV (1914), 786–96. Non-acting on Sunday seems to have been a tradition rather than the result of a specific edict. In 1606 Parliament made an effort to pass a "Keeping the Sabbath Bill," whose purpose was to prevent "Stage playes . . . upon the Sabboath dayes or sundayes," 17 February 1605/6. See HMC, MSS of the House of Lords, New Series, XI: Addenda 1514–1715 (London, 1962), pp. 96–97.

[133] An extensive examination of the days of acting from 1682 through 1692 appears in Edward A. Langhans, "New Restoration Theatre Accounts, 1682–91," Theatre Notebook, XVII (1963), 118–34. In 1683, for example, the United Company acted on 234 days, performing regularly from January through June and from October through December. During the period from June to September, however, performances occurred much more irregularly; from 16 July to 6 October, out of 72 possible acting days, plays seem to have been performed on only 14 days. In Hotson, Commonwealth and Restoration Stage, p. 308, a brief statement of the acting days from 25 March 1695 to the end of the century shows a similar distribution of acting days.

shows a possible Sunday performance, the play has been placed (in the Calendar) in a season where it will not occur on Sunday. In addition, shortly after the restoration of Charles II, Parliament decreed that each January 30 (or the day following, if that date fell on Sunday) should be strictly observed as a Fast for the martyrdom of Charles I. The theatres scheduled no plays on that date, and some Londoners considered it scandalous that dramas were sometimes acted at Court on the night preceding the Fast.[134] In addition, the companies often did not act on Wednesdays and Fridays during Lent, and Court performances ordinarily were discontinued after Shrove Tuesday.[135] But the strictness by which this custom prevailed is lessened by the fact that the theatres often permitted the "young" actors to play on Wednesdays (and sometimes on Fridays) in Lent for their own benefit. Documentation of this seeming contradiction in Lenten observance appears in two conflicting statements by Pepys in March 1667. On 1 March of that year he stated: "Friday (on which in Lent there are no plays)"; on Thursday 21 the "young men and women of the House . . . act; they having liberty to act for their own benefit on Wednesdays and Fridays this Lent."

That this practice of acting occasionally on Wednesdays and Fridays during Lent continued throughout the forty years is suggested by further examples, some of which are specifically noted in the Calendar. In the records of Nell Gwyn's attendance at the Duke's Theatre in the season of 1674–75, she on at least two occasions saw a play on a Wednesday (24 March 1674/5) or Friday (19 March 1674/5). And at the end of the century William Burnaby, in the preface to the Second Edition of *The Reformed Wife* (played at Drury Lane probably in March 1700), reported that it was first acted on a "Wednesday in Lent; for then (it seems) the Town look for a bad Entertainment." All that can be certainly stated is that the custom of a dark house on these days was irregularly observed and that there was opposition to acting on such occasions. John Evelyn argued in a letter dated 9 February 1664/5 that there should be even less frequent acting in Lent, both in the theatres and at Court.

Despite these varying practices, the playhouses regularly closed during Passion Week. No known exceptions to this practice exist. After Easter the only other holiday carefully observed was Christmas Day. Although acting seems to have resumed on the following day, lack of evidence makes uncertain whether the theatres closed on days immediately preceding Christmas.

---

[134] John Evelyn, in a letter dated 9 February 1664/5, expressed his distress that performances at that time occurred at Court.

[135] Pepys, seeing *The Wild Gallant* on 23 Feb. 1662/3, stated: "the last play that is likely to be acted at Court before Easter, because of the Lent coming in."

Other restrictions, less predictable, left the companies uncertain as to the extent of an acting season. The principal cause of long cessations was the death of a member of the royal family, but moderately subtle distinctions differentiated full mourning (with no plays) from mourning at Court which did not necessarily preclude acting in the public theatres. For example, the death of Queen Henrietta (30 August 1669) closed the playhouses until 18 October 1669, an interval of about six weeks. Fortunately for the actors, the closure occurred in a theatrically slack period. On the other hand, when the Duke of Gloucester died, 14 September 1660, the Court went into mourning for six weeks, yet Pepys saw a play (*Othello*) on 11 October 1660, only four weeks after the death of the Duke. The death of Charles II in the spring of 1685 naturally caused a long suspension, as did that of Queen Mary in 1695. At the end of the century the illness and death of another Duke of Gloucester, 29 July 1700, closed the theatres for six weeks, again during the Long Vacation.

Several different extraordinary occasions closed the theatres. The most extensive was the suspension for sixteen months following 5 June 1665 because of the Great Plague. On at least one occasion, in the summer of 1667, apparently from mid-June to mid-July, Pepys implies that the naval conflict with the Dutch darkened the theatres.[136] He fails to indicate whether this was the result of an edict from the Lord Chamberlain or simply a decision on the part of management.

Curtain time as distinguished from calendar time also varied. With the reopening of the theatres in 1660 performances began at three or three-thirty; Pepys wrote many times of his having dinner and then attending a play in mid-afternoon. A more specific statement occurs in the Prologue to *The Wild Gallant* (5 February 1662/3) when the "First Astrol. reads. A Figure of the heavenly Bodies in their several Apartments, Feb. the 5th half an hour after three after Noon." The Introduction to *The Damoiselles a la mode* (1667) suggests that essentially the same curtain time prevailed then ("'tis past three o' th' Clock, and the Play's ready to begin"). The performance generally lasted about three hours (Preface to *The Dutch Lover*, February 1673: "for almost three hours at *The Alchymist*"). Gradually curtain time moved toward the later afternoon. The Epilogue to *The She Gallants* (1695) suggests that plays began about four o'clock, and the entries in James Brydges' diary at the end of the century indicate that performances concluded by eight o'clock, suggesting a curtain time of from four to five o'clock. At the turn of the

[136] See Langhans, "New Restoration Theatre Accounts," for examples of closures and the slackened pace of acting in the summers.

century the theatres were moving toward a six to six-thirty curtain call, the time which the eighteenth century found most satisfactory.

When the companies performed at Court, the play began not long after the performance had concluded at the public theatre, but, as was sometimes true in the patent houses, the start of the play awaited the convenience of the King, by whose command the performance occurred. A play acted at Court on 17 November 1662 probably began about eight o'clock, as Pepys reported that it had concluded by eleven. One on 29 October 1666 was "done by ten o'clock" (Pepys); another on 18 December 1666 ran to midnight. On the principle that a Court performance lasted about three hours, these examples indicate that performances began anywhere from seven to perhaps eight-thirty. On these occasions the players had a full day. Although they usually did not offer the same play in the public theatre and at Court, nevertheless the major performers had a strenuous time, acting probably from three-thirty to six-thirty and, after a brief respite, performing again from seven or eight o'clock to ten or eleven.

ADMISSION

With the resumption of acting in 1660 management had to establish proper admission rates and practices. An early regulation, in fact, imposed by Sir Henry Herbert as a corrective upon the playhouses (13 October 1660) required that the Cockpit in Drury Lane alter its "unusual and unreasonable rates." It referred as a standard to "such usuall and accustomed rates only as were formerly taken at the Blackfriars by the late company of actors there."137 Within a short time the patent companies established the following basic charges: boxes 4s., pit 2s. 6d., galleries 1s. 6d. and 1s. Pepys, a methodical man in matters financial, frequently specifies the rates he paid: four shillings in an upper box, 19 October 1667, at the première of The Black Prince; twenty shillings for five persons in the boxes at The Tempest, 6 January 1667/8; and on 1 January 1667/8 he refers to the range of admission charges as outlined above.

The management, nevertheless, did not hold to uniform charges. Early in his playgoing Pepys, 16 December 1661, attended The Cutter of Coleman Street, which, although it was altered from The Guardian, the management considered a new play, because Pepys found, "It being the first time, the pay was doubled." He did not specify the rates, but is unlikely that they

137 Herbert, Dramatic Records, pp. 93–94.

went beyond 5s., 4s., 2s., 6d. and 1s. 6d. for the four sections of the house. Admission charges also rose for special occasions, such as a new and expensive operatic work. The second Epilogue to Shadwell's adaptation of *The Tempest* states: "And [Wit] must now at double Charges shine." Rumors held that Dryden's new opera, *Albion and Albanius*, in rehearsal on 1 January 1684/5, was to have the boxes priced at a guinea, the pit at a half-guinea, more than double the customary rates. At the end of the century the charges had been fairly well stabilized onto two scales (one starting at 4s. for the boxes, the other at 5s.). The bills for Lady Morley's attendance from 1696 to the end of the century indicate that she paid either four or five shillings in the boxes, the difference being determined by the nature of the production.[138]

Another phase of the admission charges which fortunately did not become a reality was a proposed tax based upon the entrance fees. At one time the Committee of the Whole of Parliament resolved to tax all admissions to the playhouses at the rate of 1s. on each box seat, 6d. for the pit, and 3d. elsewhere.[139] As attendance at the theatres was already high in terms of purchasing power, the proposal could have had a severely adverse effect upon the attendance of middle-class patrons, for the tax would have been a 25 per cent increase over the normal charges for the boxes and a 20 per cent increase in the pit.

An additional problem for both management and spectator was the mode of admission. As will be seen later (see the section on The Première), the press of persons anxious to attend the first performance of a new or revived play, especially one for which the town had great expectations, made it evident that the policy of "first-come, first-admitted" created confusion, crowding, long waiting, and disappointments. The desire to attend a first performance often required a spectator to arrive from one to three hours before curtain time. Pepys learned from experience that, if he wished to see a new play, he must constantly allow more and more time to secure a place. The spectators, of course, found means of alleviating the long wait. On 2 May 1668 Pepys, desiring to attend the première of *The Sullen Lovers*, went to Lincoln's Inn Fields at noon, hired a man to hold his place, left the theatre, ate, and returned to reclaim his seat. Similarly, at the première of *The Mulberry Garden*, 18 May 1668, although Pepys had reached the theatre before the doors opened, he found difficulty in securing a place; succeeding, however, he engaged "a boy to keep my place" and spent elsewhere the time before the curtain rose. In general, except for the aristocracy and wealthier

---

138 Hotson, *Commonwealth and Restoration Stage*, pp. 377–78.
139 See *The Bulstrode Papers* (London, 1879), I, 162.

patrons, this appears to have been the practice to the end of the century. The upper classes relied upon their more comfortable circumstances to send footmen to occupy seats until their masters could claim them at their leisure.[140]

The management also faced a multitude of less serious but nonetheless exasperating problems relating to admission. Not long after the theatres reopened, the Lord Chamberlain issued an order[141] touching upon a recurrent problem; it provided that no one, no matter what his "Quality," should "presume rudely or by force" to come into a theatre until the play was finished, notwithstanding the "pretended previledge by custome of forceing theire Entrance at the fourth or fifth Acts without Payment." On 29 October 1667 Pepys, coming late to *The English Monsieur*, was irritated at being asked to pay 4*s.* for a box with three acts finished; he refused and left the theatre. Essentially this remained an unsolved problem, and many examples illustrate the prevalence of the custom of seeing a part of a play for nothing. Davenant mentions it in the Epilogue to *The Man's the Master*, 1668. On 7 January 1667/8 Pepys saw at Lincoln's Inn Fields the last act of *The School for Compliments* without paying and hurried to Drury Lane to see free of charge an act of *1 Henry IV*. The Prologue to *Bellamira*, 12 May 1687, mentions those who "from adjacent Coffee Houses throng / At our fourth Act for a new Dance or Song," and the Prologue to *The Female Vertuoses*, 1693, refers critically to the "one-actors." The management made a partial solution to this problem with the discovery that After-Money could be collected from

---

[140] See W. J. Lawrence, "Early French Players in England," *The Elizabethan Playhouse and other Studies, First Series* (Stratford, 1912), p. 142, for an argument that it was the French who introduced into England the custom of sending footmen to hold places. This practice eventually led to one of the pernicious customs of the eighteenth century: the admission of footmen to the Upper Gallery free of charge. According to Cibber, *Apology*, I, 233-34, Christopher Rich, some time between 1695 and 1705, disturbed by the competition between Drury Lane and Lincoln's Inn Fields, allowed footmen to occupy the Upper Gallery free. Rich hoped that this gratuity would encourage more upper-class spectators to attend his theatre. According to Cibber, previously no footmen had been allowed to enter until the end of the fourth act, thus permitting them to be present to assist their masters and mistresses to their carriages.

[141] L. C. 5/138, 7 Dec. 1663, in Nicoll, *Restoration Drama*, p. 360. A printed directive dated 2 February in the twenty-sixth year of Charles II's reign spells out some of the prohibitions as well as the modes of admission: Our Will and Pleasure therefore is, and we do hereby straightly charge and command that no person of what quality soever, do presume to come into either of the said theatres before and during the time of acting, and until the plays are quite finished, without paying the price established for the respective places. And our further command is, that the money which shall be so paid by any persons for their respective places, shall not be returned again, after it is once paid, notwithstanding that such persons shall go out at any time before or during the play; and (to avoid future frauds) that none hereafter shall enter the pit, first, or upper gallery, without delivering to the respective doorkeeper the ticket or tickets which they received for their money paid at the first door (L. C. 7/3, Part I, p. 1).

those who came late and wished to see only the two last acts. (See the section on Theatrical Financing.)

Under these conditions, the collecting of admissions was not an easy or efficient task. In theory the system involved the issuance of tickets which could be collected by the doorkeepers and turned over to the treasurers. In the agreement of Davenant and his sharers (15 November 1660)[142] the receipts are to be taken in "by Ballatine, or tickettes souled for all doores and boxes," with three persons appointed to receive the money for these tickets. On 14 February 1684/5 Thomas Cross, treasurer of the Duke's Company until 1675, testified that one of his duties was "to receive the Tickets in againe from all the Dorekeepers together with such Tickets as this Deft. had delivered out during the whole time of his Receipts with the Dorekeepers of the Pitt, Galleries and Boxkeepers moneys."[143] The evidence suggests that a spectator (if he was paying at all) gave his money to a collector, who issued a ticket which was taken up by another collector. In a satiric pamphlet, *The Young Gallant's Academy* (1674), the author refers to the system: "Our Gallant (having paid his half Crown), and given the Door-keeper his Ticket presently advances himself into the middle of the Pit" (p. 56). Attending the Nursery on 24 February 1667/8, Pepys recorded how he was skillfully cheated during part of the process of admission: "I was prettily served this day at the playhouse-door, where, giving six shillings into the fellow's hand for us three, the fellow by legerdemain did convey one away, and with so much grace faced me down that I did give him but five, that, though I knew the contrary, yet I was overpowered by his so grave and serious demanding the other shilling, that I could not deny him."

For spectators who came into one section of the house and then moved to a portion having higher admission charges, the collectors had to be watchful and solicitous. In *The Tryal of Charles Lord Mohun* (1693), a nobleman, who was accused of murdering William Mountfort, the player, the testimony of John Rogers, a doorkeeper, illustrates this problem. Rogers testified concerning the entry of Lord Mohun and Captain Hill as follows:

Rogers. When I went to ask them for the overplus of the mony for coming in, because they came out of the Pit upon the Stage; he said he would not give it me, but if I brought any of our Masters, he would slit their Noses or something to that Effect.

---

[142] Herbert, *Dramatic Records*, pp. 96–100. No example of a London theatre ticket for the seventeenth century is known, but one for Smock Alley, Dublin, is recorded in W. A. Clark, *The Early Irish Stage: The Beginnings to 1720* (Oxford, 1955), pp. 107–8. See also "An Early Theatre Ticket," *Theatre Notebook*, XVIII (1963–64), 42 and opposite page 54.

[143] Hotson, *Commonwealth and Restoration Stage*, p. 368.

Mr. Att. Gen. Speak that over again.

Rogers. I asked them for mony, that they ought to pay more than the rest that were in the Pit, because they came upon the Stage.

These customs and procedures stimulated spectators and officials to pit their wits against each other. It was a game sufficiently entertaining to be reflected in Shadwell's *A True Widow*, ca. December 1678. In Act IV a door-keeper asks the men to pay.

> 4 MAN. No: I don't intend to stay.
> 2 DOOR-KEEP. So you say every day and see two or three Acts for nothing.
> 4 MAN. I'll break your Head, you Rascal.
> 1 DOOR-KEEP. Pray, Sir, pay me.
> 3 MAN. Set it down, I have no Silver about me, or bid my Man pay you.
> THEODOSIA. What, do Gentlemen run on tick for Plays?
> CARLOS. As familiarly as with their Taylors.

Much the same point was emphasized in Farquhar's *A Discourse Upon Comedy* at the end of the century: "There are a Parcel of saucy impudent Fellows about the Play-house, called Door-keepers, that can't let a Gentleman see a Play in Peace, without jogging, and nudging him every Minute. Sir, will you please to pay?—Sir, the Act's done, will you please to pay, Sir?"[144] Essentially these same difficulties with modes of admission prevailed in the early years of the next century.

---

[144] In *The Works of the Late Ingenious Mr Farquhar* (London, 1760), I, 100. The Prologue to Wycherley's *The Plain Dealer*, ca. December 1676, alluded to this practice: "'Tis but what here you spunge, and daily get; Poets, like Friends, to whom you are in Debt." The Prologue to *The Gentleman Dancing Master*, ca. November 1671, also alluded to the "ticking Gentry."

Advertising

DURING the early years of the Restoration period, the principal means of advertising plays were: (a) by posting playbills, (b) by scattering handbills or notices, (c) by oral announcements at the end of a day's performance, and (d) by word of mouth. The posted bill was the most formal and, probably, the most reliable of these modes, for new bills could quickly be printed and posted if a change of program necessitated an alteration. No playbills for the first decade of the Restoration have survived, but numerous references make reasonably clear what they contained and, in general, how they were made available to the public. First of all, they were displayed on the outside of the theatres, where passers-by could refresh their minds concerning the intended performance as they, like Samuel Pepys, debated whether to devote time and money to a play. Handbills may have been available for prospective spectators, as Pepys, as will be noted later, seems to have had available information which probably came from a bill and not from his own fund of knowledge or from conversation. In addition, playbills were posted at strategic points throughout London. Their function was aptly stated in the Epilogue to Mrs Behn's *The Rover*, Part II (ca. January 1681).

> *Poets are Kings of Wit, and you appear,*
> *A Parliament, by Play-Bill, summon'd here.*

On at least two occasions Pepys suggests how Londoners availed themselves of the bills. On Monday 24 March 1661/2, in the week preceding Easter, he stated: "I went to see if any play was acted, and I found none upon the post, it being Passion Week." On Christmas Day in 1666 he walked from his home to the Temple to see if a bill had been posted for that day, "but there, missing of any bills, concluded there was none." Occasional references in prologues, epilogues, and the text of plays suggest the prevalence of bills. In June 1660 the player coming on to speak the Prologue to *The Tamer Tamed* enters "reading the bill," and the Prologue to a revival of *The Alchemist* in December 1660 states: "Reading our Bill now pasted on the Post." The practice of posting bills continued to the end of the century, for *The Flying Post*, 22–25 June 1700, points out that the City of London wished to end this form of advertising: "The Right Honourable the Lord Mayor and Court of Alderman have ordered that no Play-house Bills be affix'd on any Post, &c. in this City; and the like Orders are resolved on in Westminster." This prohibition came at the height of the anti-stage sentiment in the closing years of the century.

The management sometimes supplemented the bills with other advertising matter. According to one contemporary,[145] tickets were thrown into gentlemen's carriages, one example reading: "At the Red Bull this day you may have Wit Without Money." *The Rehearsal Transpos'd* (1672), satirically commenting upon an author, stated: "His title page was posted and pasted up at every avenue next under the Play for that afternoon at the Kings or the Dukes House." Notifications of this kind were supplemented by announcements at the end of a performance concerning the play to be given on the following day. The few references suggest that this practice was customary and informal. When Pepys attended the Duke's Theatre, 7 March 1666/7, he noted: "Only little Mis. Davis did dance a jig after the end of the play, and there telling the next day's play." Verbal announcement was not without its humorous moments. On 15 September 1668 at the King's Theatre, Pepys saw in its initial run *The Damoiselles a la mode*, which was so unenthusiastically received that the announcement that it would be repeated amused the spectators: "So mean a thing as, when they come to say it would be acted again to-morrow, both he that said it [Beeston], and the pit fell-alaughing, there being this day not a quarter of the pit full."

Informally, of course, talk of the town kept Londoners well informed concerning theatrical offerings and gossip. In the Calendar one will find, in entries from Pepys' *Diary*, occasions on which he recorded what he had been told—sometimes by Wotton, his shoemaker, a knowledgeable man—about plays and players. A puff by word of mouth was recorded by Pepys on 18 October 1662: "Young Killigrew did so commend 'The Villaine,' a new play made by Tom Porter, and acted only on Saturday at the Duke's house, as if there never had been any such play come upon the stage."

Although no bills from the earliest years of the Restoration have survived, one can reconstruct essentially what they contained. A specific example is in *The Adventures of Five Hours*, 8 January 1662/3: "The Prologue Enters with a Play-Bill in his hand, and reads: 'This Day being the 15th of December, shall be Acted a New Play, never Plai'd before, call'd The Adventures of Five Hours.'" In all probability bills at this time contained the date (minus the year), the name of the theatre, the title of the play, whether

145 Hotson, *Commonwealth and Restoration Stage*, pp. 34, 67.

it was new or a revival, and, if a revived work, how long it had been off the stage. Pepys frequently referred to plays in such fashion as to suggest that some of his information came from playbills. Seeing *The Country Captain* on 26 October 1661, he stated that it had not been acted for twenty-five years, and he made the same point on 23 January 1666/7, when he stayed after a performance and learned that next day would be acted *The Goblins*, "a play of Suckling's, not acted these twenty-five years." On 3 March 1668/9 at *The Lady's Trial*, he stated: "The first time acted these forty years." As it is very unlikely that Pepys would have this kind of information at the tip of his tongue, he presumably learned it from a bill. Similarly, his statement concerning *Cupid's Revenge*, 17 August 1668, that the play was "This day the first time acted here" implies a written or oral announcement preceding the performance, as the Prologue to *Wits Led by the Nose*, June 1677, also emphasizes.

> *A Play Bill discover'd upon the Door*
> *What's here? never Acted before.*

During the years from 1660 to 1700 the make-up of the playbill apparently did not materially alter. The basic similarity of the extant bills is evident in an account of the surviving ones published by Ifan Kyrle Fletcher.[146] The ten for the years preceding 1700 name the theatre, the title of the play (sometimes with a headnote such as "Not Acted these 16 Years") and admonitory statements: "No Person to stand on the Stage." No extant bill lists a cast, and references to the author apparently did not occur until late in the century. John Dryden, writing on 4 March 1698/9, stated that he had seen William Congreve's name on a bill for *The Double Dealer*, adding, "but the printing an Authors name, in a Play Bill, is a new manner of proceeding, at least in England."[147] During these forty years the management also printed some bills in red instead of black, a custom possibly introduced into England by the French, as Dryden's Prologue to *Arviragus* (1672–1674) implies.

> *A Brisk French Troop is grown your dear delight,*
> *Who with broad bloody Bills call you each day.*

As red bills existed in the early eighteenth century, occasional ones may have appeared before 1700.

In spite of the growing popularity of periodicals, some issued twice weekly, others weekly or monthly, the managers of the theatres did not

---

[146] "British Playbills before 1718," *Theatre Notebook*, XVII (1962–63), 28–50.
[147] *The Letters of John Dryden*, ed. C. E. Ward (Durham, North Carolina, 1942), p. 113.

regularly print notices in the journals as a supplement to the bills, although the proprietors of concert halls early began to insert advertisements in the *London Gazette* and elsewhere. The theatres found, however, an unofficial medium of information in Peter Motteux's *The Gentleman's Journal* in the 1690's, for Motteux liberally commented upon plays, gave reports of forthcoming attractions, printed songs from dramas, and discussed the response of London to new plays. But a monthly publication was not a suitable medium for announcements of daily performances, and it was not until the end of the century when more frequent issues (not yet daily) of the *Post Boy* and *Post Man* appeared that the managers occasionally inserted bills in these newspapers. The contrast between a playbill of the last decade and a newspaper notice at the end of the century may be seen in these two examples. The first is a bill.[148]

Never Acted but Once
At the THEATRE ROYALL, in
Drury-Lane, this present *Wensday* being
the Nineth day of *November*, [1692] will be presented
A New Play called
HENRY the Second King of England.
No Money to be return'd after the curtain
is drawn. By their Majesties Servants.
Vivant Rex & Regina.

The second is an insertion in the *Flying Post*, 2–4 July 1700.

At the Request, and for the Entertainment of several Persons of Quality, at the New Theatre in Lincolns-Inn-Fields, to Morrow, being Friday, the 5th of this instant July, will be acted, The Comical History of Don Quixote, both Parts being made into one by the Author. With a new Entry by the little Boy, being his last time of Dancing before he goes to France; Also Mrs Elford's new Entry, never performed but once; and Miss Evan's Jigg and Irish Dance. With several new Comical Dances, compos'd and perform'd by Monsieur L'Sec and others. Together with a new Pastoral Dialogue, by Mr Gorge, and Mrs Haynes; and variety of other Singing. It being for the Benefit of a Gentleman in great distress; and for the Relief of his Wife and three Children.

[148] This bill is in Verney MSS., HMC, Seventh Report, p. 509, and has been reproduced in W. J. Lawrence, *The Elizabethan Playhouse and Other Studies, Second Series* (Stratford, 1913), p. 81, and opposite page 240.

The RED BULL PLAYHOUSE, with celebrated characters from Elizabethan drama shown on the platform stage. *From a print in the Harvard Library.*

The LORD CHAMBERLAIN'S WARRANT of 3 January 1670/71 for payment to the Duke of York's Company for performances attended by Charles II. *From the original document, now in the Harvard Library.*

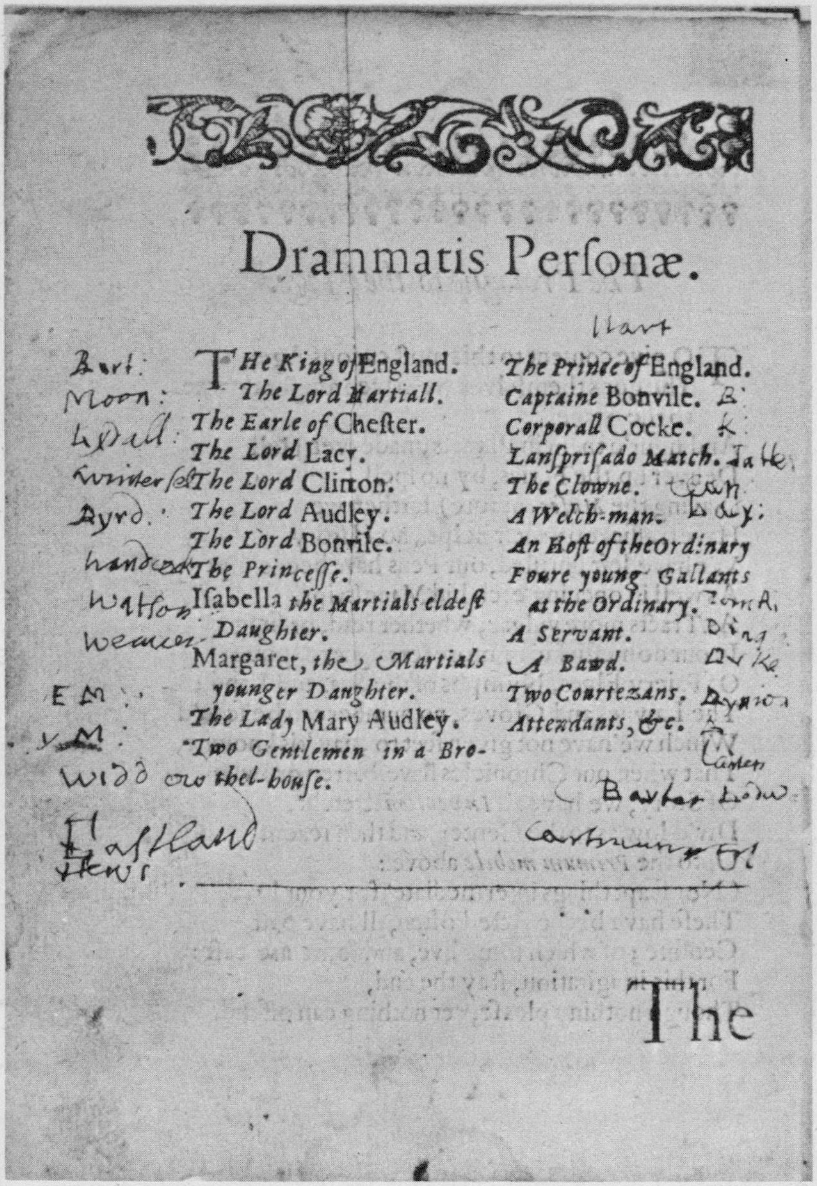

Drammatis Personæ.

Hart

The King of England.   *The Prince of England.*
        The Lord Martiall.   Captaine Bonvile.
The Earle of Chester.   Corporall Cocke.
The Lord Lacy.   Lansprisado Match.
The Lord Clinton.   The Clowne.
The Lord Audley.   A Welch-man.
The Lord Bonvile.   An Hoft of the Ordinary
The Princeſſe.   Foure young Gallants
Isabella *the* Martials eldeſt   at the Ordinary.
    Daughter.   A Servant.
Margaret, *the* Martials   A Bawd.
    younger Daughter.   Two Courtezans.
The Lady Mary Audley.   Attendants, &c.
Two Gentlemen in a Bro-
    thel-house.

(handwritten marginal names:) Bart. Moon: Lydell Winterſel Byrd. handcok Watſon Weaver E M: Y M: Widd Haſtland Hews

(handwritten right-side names:) B. K. Ja Hq. Loy: Tomk: Dicken Duke Dynio Carleſs Baxter Low Cartwright &c.

The

His Majesties Bill owing to the Duke of Yorks Theatre
from November 16th 1668 till June 20th 1670.

		£		
1668 November 16th.	At Court, Sir Martin	20	0	0
November 30.	At Court, The Changeling	20	0	0
Decemb: 8.	At the Theatre, Tryphon	10	0	0
Decemb: 14.	At Court, Woemen pleas'd	20	0	0
Decemb: 21.	At the Theatre, Macbeth	10	0	0
Decemb: 28.	At Court, Tryphon	20	0	0
Decemb: 29.	At the Theatre, Th Impertinents, the King and Quien	20	0	0
February 1.	At Court, the Guardian	20	0	0
February 15.	At Court, The Adventures	20	0	0
February 19.	At the Theatre, the Tempest	10	0	0
February 25.	At the Theatre, the Royall Shipherdis	10	0	0
1669 March 30.	At the Theatre, Love in a Tubb	10	0	0
April 15.	At the Theatre, Guzman	10	0	0
April 24.	At the Theatre, Sir Martin	10	0	0
June 14.	At the Theatre, the Hypocrite	10	0	0
Dec: 14.	At the Theatre, M: Antony	10	0	0
Jan: 7.	At the Theatre, the Gintleman of Venice	10	0	0
Jan: 12.	At the Theatre, the Sophy	10	0	0
Feb: 19.	At the Theatre, the Woman made a Justice	10	0	0
Feb: 24.	At the Theatre, the Woman made a Justice	10	0	0
March 10.	At the Theatre, the Gamister	10	0	0
1670. May 9.	At the Theatre, Ji Solomon	10	0	0
June 20.	At the Theatre, Shee woud if she coud	10	0	0
	Total	300	0	0

H: Harris

A SCHEDULE OF PLAYS attended by Charles II. From the original document signed
by the actor-manager Henry Harris and now located in the *Harvard Library*.

The comedienne NELL GWYNN. P. Van Bleeck's mezzotint from the painting by
Peter Lely. *Courtesy of the Harvard Library.*

The MOORISH DANCE, in Act II, Scene 1, of Elkanah Settle's *The Empress of Morocco*
From an engraving in the 1673 edition.

TORTURE SCENE from Act V of *The Empress of Morocco*. *From the engraving in the 1673 edition.*

The character actor JOHN LACY in three favorite rôles. *From a copy of the etching by W. Hopkins in the Harvard Library.*

The Benefit

THE THEORY and practice of the Benefit are not explicitly revealed during the years from 1660 to 1700, yet the principal customs concerning it evolved into the more formalized practices of the eighteenth century. Like many theatrical traditions, the Benefit, never established definitively by edict, gradually took form. During this period, it evolved in five ways, for the (a) actresses as a group, (b) the "young" actors, (c) the individual performer, (d) the dramatist, and (e) charity. During the ten years (1660–69) of Pepys' *Diary* the theatres occasionally permitted the women of the house a yearly performance for their own profit. On 28 September 1668, at Drury Lane, Pepys reported: "Knepp's maid comes to me, to tell me that the women's day at the playhouse is to-day, and that therefore I must be there, to increase their profit [at] *The City Match* . . . the house, for the women's sake, mighty full." The Prologue to *The French Conjurer* (ca. June 1677) speaks of it as "The Women's Play," suggesting that it was produced for the actresses' annual benefit. Elkanah Settle, observing the lack of success for his new play, *The Ambitious Slave* (21 March 1693/4), and little hope for a good benefit for himself on the third day "made a present of it to the women in the house." Although evidence for the women's benefit is scanty, it may have been related to several performances in which women only acted, a custom also prevailing in the first decade of the eighteenth century. Nevertheless, this type of benefit lost favor when individuals secured personal benefits, perhaps because of difficulty in distributing the profits from a multiple benefit equitably.

Another practice which prevailed in the 1660's but which did not persist long in the same form was the privilege accorded the young actors of playing on Wednesdays and Fridays in Lent for their own profit. Just why this violation of nonacting on these days was countenanced is not clear, but it may have been considered partially an "amateur" performance. (For examples, see Management and Operations.)[149] Presumably these actors paid the customary Daily Charge and divided the profits among themselves. This

[149] For a discussion of this practice, see Philip H. Gray, Jr., "Lenten Casts and the Nursery," *PMLA*, LIII (1938), 781–94.

custom changed in the 1680's and 1690's to allow the young actors to play during the summer. Although this was usually a slack season, they could plan the summer's entire offerings instead of intermingling their occasional productions with the main repertory in Lent. Two sets of memoranda[150] point to the regularity with which the companies allowed the less experienced performers full possession of the stage from mid-June to mid-September, and a bill for Drury Lane 8 July 1700 (see the Calendar) exemplifies the practice.

The origin of benefits for individual actors is not known. Colley Cibber stated, however, that the first person to receive an individual benefit was Elizabeth Barry, an event he placed in the reign of King James (1685–88), but he added that this did not become a custom until the division of the company in the season of 1694–95.[151] Evidence concerning individual benefits for that season appears in the Petition of the Players (ca. December 1694) and the reply of the Patentees.[152] According to these memoranda, Mrs Barry usually had a benefit each year, Betterton (when on salary) had an annual present of fifty guineas (comparable to a benefit), and Mrs Bracegirdle had demanded a benefit for herself. Following the break between the two groups (Rich-Skipwith and Betterton-Mrs Barry-Mrs Bracegirdle) in the season of 1694–95, proposed articles for the Patentees' company specify the arrangements for benefits.[153] Dogget, for example, was to have the benefit of one old play acted on a Wednesday or Friday in Lent, he to pay the charges. Because several other agreements at this time do not specify benefits, Rich apparently used them as lures to attract actors whom he seriously needed, the custom having not yet achieved the status of a regular privilege. At Betterton's house, the actor-sharers, distributing the profits among themselves, did not need regularly to offer this privilege. Nevertheless, the principle of a benefit for an actor had been substantially established by the end of the seventeenth century, and the next century made it a customary part of nearly every contract between performer and management.

During this period the dramatist's benefit was probably the most important one, for not only did it prevail earlier than the actors' benefit, but it was obviously the main source of revenue for the professional dramatist. Without a benefit, he had only the gifts of his patron and the profits from the sale of his play, neither source being wholly lucrative or dependable. So long

[150] See Langhans, "New Restoration Theatre Accounts," pp. 118–34, and Hotson, *Commonwealth and Restoration Stage*, pp. 308–9.

[151] *Apology*, I, 161.

[152] Nicoll, *Restoration Drama*, pp. 368–79.

[153] *Ibid.*, pp. 383–84.

as the dramatist was titled or a gentleman of means, he might write without concern for financial gain, as scribbling was his avocation. This was not, however, the case with the professional man of letters, such as Dryden, Shadwell, Settle, Wycherley, or Congreve, to whom the stage was a welcome source of income. As a result, the practice developed of allowing the playwright the receipts (above the House Charges) on the third night, the privilege sometimes extending to the sixth and ninth performances in the initial run. Although the gift of the third day's net receipts began early, it is uncertain when the sixth day's benefit became firm. The Preface to Aphra Behn's *The Lucky Chance* (ca. April 1686) declares: "I am not content to write for a Third day only," yet in the spring of 1688 the emphasis fell primarily upon the third day. In April of that year John Crowne thanked the King for his attendance at the third performance of *Darius*, and in May Shadwell emphasized the generosity of his friends on the third day, neither referring to a possible or actual benefit at the sixth performance. On the other hand, Southerne in the Dedication to *Sir Anthony Love* (ca. September 1690) refers to "the Third and the Sixth," suggesting a double benefit, and Vanbrugh in *The Provok'd Wife* (ca. May 1697) states: "The Third day is for us—Nay, and the Sixt." The point is made emphatic in the Prologue to Charles Hopkins' *Boadicea* (ca. November 1697).

> *Do you not wonder, Sirs, in these poor Days,*
> *Poets should hope for Profit from their Plays?*
> *Dream of a full Third Day, nay, good sixth Night.*

As these arrangements evolved, the dramatist first of all hoped that his play would not be damned at the première. Even if it had a lukewarm reception at the beginning, he could augment the attendance on the third day by solicitation, directly by himself or with the assistance of friends. As *A Lash for the Parable Makers* (1691) stated: "But tho' the House were not so well filled at the first opening, you may be sure at their next meeting it was crowded like a Play-House upon the Poets day" (p. 2). In the Dedication to *Theodosius* (ca. September 1680) Lee thanked the Duchess of Richmond for bringing to the theatre the Princess, "whose single Presence on the Poet's day is a Subsistence for him all the Year after." An example of solicitation is the third performance of Dennis's *Iphigenia* (late 1699), when Colonel Codrington, who wrote the Epilogue, prevailed upon his friends to take tickets for the dramatist's benefit.[154] The practice had its virtues and defects. It could be very lucrative, as was Shadwell's benefit for *The Squire of*

---

[154] *A Life of John Dennis* (London, 1734).

f

Alsatia, 3 May 1688, which, according to Downes,[155] brought him £130 on the third day, £16 more than any previous dramatist had received. Southerne received £140 at his benefit for *The Fatal Marriage* (ca. February 1693/4), £50 additional from noblemen, and £36 for the play from the publisher. The lure of the benefit, however, bred occasional satiric thrusts at would-be playwrights. The Preface to John Dryden Jr's *The Husband His Own Cuckold* (ca. 1695) argued that some men assume "the name of Poet, who never had any other call to that Art besides the hope of a third day."

The most detailed arrangements for a benefit are the negotiations for the production of Cibber's *Woman's Wit* (29 October 1696).[156] He was to pay the house charges on the third day; if the receipts at the following performance were at least £40, the drama would be offered a fifth time. If the income on that day came to £40, Cibber would receive the receipts (less the charges) on the sixth offering. If the box office brought in £40 on that day, the comedy would be acted a seventh time; and if the receipts then rose to £50, the charges assessed on the sixth day would be returned to Cibber. Obviously it was to the author's advantage to secure a good attendance throughout the initial run.

The dramatist might make other arrangements. He could become a sharer, as were Dryden and Settle in the King's Company. As a sharer, Dryden bound himself to write three plays yearly; in 1677 the players alleged that for his share and a quarter Dryden had received £300 or £400 yearly even though he had sometimes produced only one play each year. Nevertheless, at the acting of *All for Love*, the King's Company granted him a benefit on his third day.[157] Later, no longer a sharer, he estimated that by revising Robert Howard's *The Conquest of China by the Tartars*, he could secure £100 by a benefit. In 1700 rumor held that his assistance in revising *The Pilgrim* brought the third day's gain to his estate. Other playwrights, particularly Thomas D'Urfey and Elkanah Settle, appear at times to have been either sharers or so closely attached to a single company as to have similar status. Another perquisite of minor financial importance—free admittance to the playhouse—was granted to some dramatists. Upon the great success of *The Old Batchelor* Congreve received this privilege. This practice created some amusement, for Farquhar, in *An Essay on Comedy* (1702) lampooned a gallant who intended to write a play so that he might "enjoy the Freedom of the House."

155 *Roscius Anglicanus*, p. 41.
156 Nicoll, *Restoration Drama*, pp. 381–82.
157 *Ibid.*, p. 329.

On the other hand, the benefit often was a disappointment, even a disaster. When Cibber revised *Richard III* (ca. December 1699) he ruefully confessed (in the Preface to *Ximena*, 1719) that he did not gain even £5 from it at his benefit. The three commentators in *A Comparison Between the Two Stages* (1702) amused themselves with the dilemma of the dramatist who not only saw the house charges of £34 consume a large portion of the third day's receipts but also got bills for "Gloves, for Chocolet, for Snuff; this Singer begg'd a Guinea, that Dancer the same."[158]

The Charitable Benefit occurred only sporadically. No particular precedent seems to have determined this type, yet it occurs before 1700 most frequently in times of theatrical stress. The purported offer of the companies to contribute to charity in 1666 in return for permission to reopen the theatres before the Plague had fully subsided is a case in point. Similarly, at the end of the century, when the playhouses came under scrutiny for their alleged licentiousness, the companies staged benefits for public causes. At the end of June 1700 both houses contributed their "whole Profits" (*London Post*, 28 June–1 July 1700) for the relief of the English enslaved at Machanisso in Barbary. On 5 July 1700 Lincoln's Inn Fields offered *Don Quixote* for a "Gentleman in great Distress; and for the Relief of his Wife and Three Children." These sentimental gestures persisted into the next century.

[158] Pp. 8–9.

Scenes, Machines, Properties, Costumes, and Lighting

SCENES AND MACHINES

SIR WILLIAM DAVENANT brought to the Restoration a profound interest in augmenting the effectiveness of dramatic presentations with movable and changeable scenery and with devices, commonly called "machines," for creating rapid and sometimes startling illusions and eye-catching risings and descents of chariots, angels, tables, and other objects. His regard for decorative spectacle had shown itself in the entertainments he presented privately in the decade before 1660, and, as soon as he had established himself in the theatre in Lincoln's Inn Fields, he put his theories into practice. Nearly all the commentators of his day stress his leadership in bringing changeable scenery into fuller use in the professional theatres.[159] For the majority of spectators, the concept of scenic embellishment, particularly the use of changeable scenes, was new; and commentators clearly show that these innovations attracted much attention and impressed many spectators. In fact, one result of Davenant's lead was imitation by the King's Company. Although Killigrew's company could not make extensive use of scenes in 1660, because it lacked the proper facilities, it followed Davenant's direction when it opened and equipped the new Theatre Royal in Drury Lane.[160] This development as a regular feature of the public stage is an important one. As noted by W. J. Lawrence and Richard Southern, evidence for its appearance in special private performances dates from as early as 1574, but application to the public stage begins with Davenant. The Restoration revived the living theatre, in which the quality of the dramatic text is largely determined by the staging of the show. Davenant's purpose involved the conception that "the changing of scenes was intended to be visible; it was part of the show; it came into existence purely to be watched."[161]

When Pepys attended performances at Davenant's theatre in Lincoln's Inn Fields in 1661 he was properly impressed with the scenes. At *The Siege of*

[159] See *Historia Histrionica* (1699), in Cibber's *Apology*, I, xxii; and Downes, *Roscius Anglicanus*, p. 20.

[160] In Cibber, *Apology*, I, xxxiii.

[161] Southern, *Changeable Scenery*, pp. 17–25.

Rhodes, 2 July 1661, an operatic work with scenic effects, he commented: "The scene opened; which indeed is very fine and magnificent." Similarly at *The Wits*, 15 August 1661, he found the scenes "admirable," and his response to *Hamlet*, 24 August 1661, stressed that it was "done with scenes very well," as though the use of scenery for dramas of this nature was new to him. The creator of the early scenery for Davenant is not known, but it is worth noting that in the autumn of 1660 the Italians were considered the best scene designers,[162] and that Charles II once considered allowing Giulio Gentileschie to build a theatre, import Italian musicians, and prepare scenes and music for Italian opera.[163] Although nothing came of this project, the attempt is evidence of a sense of excitement over innovations, scenes, and spectacle. In addition, Davenant's concern with scenic effects showed itself in his early provision for a scene room, for on 16 January 1660/1 he acquired space for one.

Competitively, the King's Company could not resist the trend toward scenic innovations. For its opening play in its new theatre, *The Humorous Lieutenant*, 7 May 1663, Pepys especially noted that it was acted "with scenes." Thereafter, the two companies vied equally in the variety and lavishness of their scenic adornments. When Pepys attended *The Faithful Shepherdess* at the King's on 13 June 1663, he disliked the play, but added that it was "yet much thronged after, and often shown, but it is only for the scenes' sake, which is very fine indeed and worth seeing." Evelyn, at the same theatre on 5 February 1663/4 to see *The Indian Queen*, a lavish operatic work, emphasized that it was "so beautiful with rich scenes, as the like had never ben seene here as haply (except rarely any where else) on a mercenarie theatre." (In the printed version, Act v is described: "The Scene opens, and discovers the Temple of the Sun all of Gold, and four Priests in habits of white and red Feathers attending by a bloody Altar.") When scenery, costumes, and spectacle were handsomely harmonized, Pepys was visually pleased, as he emphasized at a production of *Heraclius*, 8 March 1663/4: "At the drawing up of the curtaine, there was the finest scene of the Emperor and his people about him, standing in their fixed and different postures in their Roman habits, above all that ever I yet see at any of the theatres."

What was the nature of the "scenes" in a production? In the first place, Davenant developed the principle of having the curtain drawn after the

---

[162] See S. A. Strong, *A Catalogue of Letters and other Historical Documents* (London, 1903), pp. 293–94.

[163] Hotson, *Commonwealth and Restoration Stage*, p. 177, and Boswell, *Restoration Court Stage*, pp. 114–15.

speaking of the Prologue, revealing a "scene" (Pepys' record of the opening of *Heraclius* is an effective example). The curtain stayed open until after the speaking of the Epilogue. From Prologue to Epilogue, then, all changes of "scenes" took place in full view of the audience in the sense that a "scene" represents a particular grouping of the three principal forms: side scenes (wings), shutters, and "relieve" scenes.[164] Davenant used changeable scenery not primarily to coincide with changes in the dramatic action; "it is scenery in the stage sense of the decking of a stage, but not scenery in the landscape sense of a background seen behind people."[165] Southern visualizes the stage in these terms: "a form with a deep forestage, flanked by entrance doors in the proscenium sides, and standing in front of an 'inner' stage which was primarily intended as a scenic area and possibly less as an acting area—the acting area being mainly confined to the forestage."[166] By means of grooves—certainly three sets, perhaps four—and the back-scene as well as wings a series of "scenes" could be quickly created. Thus, the statement in the dramatic text reading "the scene opens" means that the scenery actually moved and the statement "the scene closes" refers to the drawing together of the two halves of the back-scene. These occur at transitions within the play, the opening and closing of the curtain occurring only to frame the entire dramatic dialogue.[167] To permit a rapid succession of "scenes," the successive shutters were placed far enough apart to allow one "scene" to disclose, on opening, a group in front of another shutter scene. A bare stage ordinarily indicated the end of an act. In the early years following 1660 this interval may have been brief and possibly filled with "act-tunes" played by the orchestra. The theatres, however, soon seized upon the bare stage to introduce entr'acte entertainments; by the end of the century the audience expected to be amused during the intervals in the "scene" by song, dance, and, occasionally, musical interludes.

To execute these changes of "scene" the theatres employed scenekeepers and machinists, who stood ready to manipulate the pieces of scenery in the grooves. The manuscript of *The Change of Crownes*, acted on 15 April 1667, has marginal notations such as "1st whistle ready" (Act I), "2d whistle ready" (Act II), "ffirst whistle ready" (Act III), presumably representing

[164] For a discussion of some of these technical matters, see Southern, *Changeable Scenery*, pp. 19-20, 120-22, and Lee J. Martin, "From Forestage to Proscenium," *Theatre Survey*, IV (1963), 3-28, particularly pp. 3-5.

[165] Southern, *Changeable Scenery*, pp. 114-15.

[166] *Ibid.*, p. 119. Martin, "From Forestage to Proscenium," pp. 23-24, argues that, contrary to the view of some theatrical historians, a fair proportion of the dialogue was spoken from within the "scene" rather than on the forestage.

[167] Southern, *Changeable Scenery*, p. 126.

signals to the scenekeepers to prepare to make the change.[168] By 1690 the
stage hands apparently had another device: a painted canvas dropped from
above, perhaps by rollers, similar to a curtain. References to this appear in
The Prophetess.[169] The workmen assisting in scenic illusions also had at their
command "machines," a term commonly employed for those flyings and
moving objects within sight of the audience; these were manipulated by
"engines." The editors of the California edition of Dryden's plays note that
for *The Rival Ladies* apparently the machinists had available two machines for
"swift motion" and two "slow machines" (p. 311). The dances masked some
of the manipulations which were not part of the visual display.

Numerous examples attest to the attention given to "scenes" and the
means by which they were made impressive. When Pepys had a chance to
inspect Drury Lane, 19 March 1664/5, while it was closed by the Plague, he
found "the paintings very pretty." Prince Cosmo III, traveling in England,
visited the theatres: "The scenery is very light, capable of a great many
changes, and embellished with beautiful landscapes."[170] When Dorset
Garden was in construction, Evelyn, 26 June 1671, stopped "to see the new
Machines for the intended Scenes, which were indeede very costly, &
magnificent." The Epilogue to *Mr Anthony*, 14 December 1669 (see also the
Epilogue to Cartwright's *The Ordinary*), satirically comments upon the role
these devices played in appealing to audiences.

> *Damn'd Plays shall be adorn'd with mighty Scenes,*
> *And Fustian shall be spoke in huge Machines;*
> *And we will purling Streams and Fireworks show,*
> *And you may live to see it Rain and Snow.*

Or, as Dryden stated in an Epilogue to the University of Oxford, July 1673:

> *But when all fail'd, to strike the Stage quite Dumb,*
> *Those wicked Engines call'd Machines are come.*
> *Thunder and Lightning now for Wit are Play'd.*

Commentators and the texts of plays make abundant references to special
effects. Pepys, seeing *Catiline* on 19 December 1668, referred to "a fine scene
of the Senate, and of a fight, that ever I saw in my life," and in *The Island
Princess* on 7 January 1668/9 "a good scene of a town on fire." A concentration
upon scenic and mechanic embellishment shows also in Thomas Shadwell's

---

168 *The Change of Crownes*, ed. Frederick S. Boas (London, 1949), pp. 23, 39, 54.
169 Southern, *Changeable Scenery*, pp. 164, 167.
170 *Travels of Cosmo the Third*, pp. 190–91.

alteration of *The Tempest* in the winter of 1674–75. In Act I the stage directions call for a "noble Arch, supported by large wreathed Columns of the Corinthian Order," and behind them them the "Scene represents a thick Cloudy Sky, a very Rocky Coast, and a Tempestuous Sea in perpetual Agitation." In the same Act, during streaks of lightning and claps of thunder, "horrid Shapes flying down amongst the Sailors" contributed to the atmosphere. In Act II "a Devil rises," and in Act V the audience saw "Ariel flying from the Sun, [advancing] toward the Pit." The most elaborate devices were used in Act IV: "A Table rises, and four Spirits with Wine and Meat enter, placing it, as they dance, on the Table: The Dance ended, the Bottles vanish, and the Table sinks again." This scene so impressed Downes, the prompter, that he referred to it as a fine example of legerdemain: "particularly, one Scene Painted with Myriads of Ariel Spirits; and another flying away, with a Table Furnisht out with Fruits, Sweetmeats and all sorts of Viands; just when Duke Trinculo and his Companions, were going to Dinner."[171]

A short time later the Duke's Theatre used similar devices in Shadwell's *Psyche*, 24 February 1674/5. The Preface to the printed text frankly states the aim of spectacle: "The great Design was to entertain the Town with variety of Musick, curious Dances, splendid Scenes and Machines." To this end, the company engaged Matthew Locke to compose the vocal music, Giovanni Baptista Draghi to create the instrumental; for the dances the management brought St. André and other performers from France, and engaged one Stephenson to design the scenery. Among the devices were ascents and descents: In Act I "Six Furies arise" and "Furies sink." Later Venus "descends in her Chariot, drawn with Doves," and "Venus ascends." In Act II, "The Earth opens, infernal Spirits rise . . . Two Zephiri descend and take Psyche by each Arm, and fly into the Clouds with her. Cupid descends a little way, hanging in the Air." In Act III the "Furies descend and strike the Altar, and break it, and every one flies away with a fire brand in's hand." In Act V Venus descends in her chariot, then mounts it and flies away, with a finale: "Venus being almost lost in the Clouds. Cupid flies up and gets into the Chariot, and brings her back." Pepys had enjoyed this type of illusion in *The Humorous Lieutenant*, 23 February 1666/7: "only the Spirit in it that grows very tall, and then sinks again to nothing, having two heads breeding upon one." *The Lancashire Witches*, ca. November 1681, made extensive use of similar techniques. After thunder and lightning in Act I, "One of the Witches flies away with the Candle and Lanthorn, Mother Demdike sets him

---

[171] *Roscius Anglicanus*, pp. 34–35. It was this kind of display which, incorporated into pantomime, delighted the audiences of the next century.

upon the Top of a Tree, and they all fly away Laughing." In Act II the Witches have "Their Brooms all march off and fetch Bottles." The vogue of spectacle, illusion, and dexterity brought a melancholy response from the author of the Epilogue to *Love in the Dark*, 10 May 1675.

> *For Songs and Scenes, a double Audience bring,*
> *And Doggrel takes, which Smiths in Sattin sing.*
> *Now to Machines, and a dull Mask you run,*
> . . . .
> *Players turn Puppets now at your desire,*
> *In their Mouth's Nonsence, in their Tails a Wire,*
> *They fly through Clouds of Clouts, and showers of fire.*

In the second Epilogue to Shadwell's *The Tempest* the speaker succinctly praises the achievements of the company: "We have Machines to some perfection brought." In achieving this goal, the managers secured new personnel, especially scene designers, scenekeepers, and machinists. A few of these men received sufficient recognition from their contemporaries to be known to us. Isaac Fuller created the scenes for Dryden's *Tyrannic Love*, ca. 24 June 1669, for which he gained, after litigation, £335 10s. for his talents and labor.[172] In the season of 1670–71 Robert Streeter prepared for *The Conquest of Granada* what Evelyn described as "very glorious scenes & perspectives." As already pointed out, one Stephenson designed the settings for *Psyche*. Richard Rider, the King's Carpenter, created those for the magnificently staged *Calisto*. At the end of the century Robert Robinson contracted with the Drury Lane company for several "sets of Scenes & Machines" for a new opera by Elkanah Settle, for which he was to be paid £130.[173] Other designers known by name are John Webb, Robert Aggas, and Samuel Powers.

Just how many scenekeepers a company employed is not known, but extant records suggest that from eight to twelve may have been on duty simultaneously. In a recent article listing the personnel in the Lord Chamberlain's Registers, John Harold Wilson notes twelve names sworn in as "Scenekeeper" for His Majesty's Theatre (presumably the King's Company) from 12 July 1664 through 29 June 1665: Antonio Brunnati, Robert Moseley, Anthony Moore, Henry Wright, William Edwards, John Gilbert, Edward Hartley, Simon Horne, John Preston, Thomas Cordell, Thomas Elrington, Emmanuell Fonesca.[174] Many of these men appear on later rolls, with new

---

[172] Hotson, *Commonwealth and Restoration Stage*, pp. 250–53. This large sum represented payment for six weeks of work.

[173] L. C. 7/3, in Nicoll, *Restoration Drama*, p. 344.

[174] "Players' Lists in the Lord Chamberlain's *Registers*," *Theatre Notebook*, XVIII (1963), 28.

ones added from time to time, but no list makes perfectly clear the total employed in a single season. At the end of the century a list of the company at Lincoln's Inn Fields, 20 July 1695,[175] refers to "The 4 scene keepers," and it is possible that the smallness of this theatre, coupled with its reluctance to produce spectacles, may have required fewer such employees than were necessary for operatic works. Individuals designated as machinists or working with machines are John Guipponi, William Taimes, and Thomas Wright.[176] One assumes that the division of labors between scenekeepers and machinists was not yet so well established as to preclude the probability that some of the scenekeepers doubled as machinists. Probably they also served as supernumeraries, for in the satiric play, *The Female Wits*, ca. 1696, in Act I the "Scene-keeper" speaks a line.

PROPERTIES

Information concerning properties, apart from scenery, machinery, and costumes, for use on the stage is relatively scarce, although a good many extant orders concern performances at Court. Numerous plays, of course, call for properties, but the documents which reveal usage are usually missing. Nevertheless, Pepys tells us a little about properties. During the Plague, on 19 March 1665/6, he stopped in at the darkened Bridges Street playhouse, and in the property room saw "here a wooden-leg, there a ruff, here a hobby-horse, there a crown," and mused on the contrast between these inert objects and the fine show they made on the stage. An occasional order indicates preparations for a performance, such as one for *Sir Courtly Nice*, to be given at Court on 30 April 1690, calling for a large looking glass. The text of the play indicates how the properties were to be utilized: "Enter two Bravoes, and hang up a great Picture of Angelica's against the Balcony, and two little ones at each side of the Door" (Act II). For a performance of *Hyde Park*, 11 July 1668, Pepys noted that "horses are brought upon the stage" to lend realism. A warrant dated 10 April 1690 calls for a cushion "of Gold Coloured Damaske," a "table Carpett of the like Damaske four foote long and two foot three Inches broad," and a "Pewter Standish," but does not specify the play.[177] In discussing how "scenes" opened to reveal a new setting, L. J. Martin points out some of the properties required in scenes of plays he

[175] Sybil Rosenfeld, "Unpublished Stage Documents," *Theatre Notebook*, XI (1957), 94.
[176] See Wilson, "Players' Lists in the Lord Chamberlain's *Registers*," pp. 28–29, and Nicoll, *Restoration Drama*, p. 44.
[177] L. C. 5/138, p. 49, in Nicoll, *Restoration Drama*, p. 380.

studied.[178] For *The Round-Heads*, ca. December 1681, the settings require a table, chairs, and papers for a Council Chamber (III, i); candles, lights, a full-curtained bed, and probably a table (IV, i); a canopy, a table with bottles and glasses (IV, iii). For *An Old Troop* (ca. 1663) Scene 1 of Act IV calls for a "Taffeta bed" with cushions to be thrown about the scene.

Some of the properties listed in extant orders obviously were for immediate consumption. A document for a performance at Court on 31 October 1666 concerns food for consumption at rehearsal and on stage: 12 quarts of "Sack," 12 of "Clarett," 8 gallons of beer, 12 loaves of "Whitebread," 12 of "Brown bread." Other supplies assisted the meal: 12 "White Dishes to Drincke in," 2 "Bombards" to fetch beer, 24 torches for illumination, 4 baskets of "Cole" for fires, and 4 pounds of tallow candles.[179] As a performance at Court sometimes followed closely upon one at the theatre, the comedians may have needed a meal during the interval, but many plays called for real or pretended meals on stage. No doubt, the theatres had on their rolls individuals whose primary function was the securing and preservation of properties, but the extant lists fall to specify this class. In the lists of comedians examined by John Harold Wilson appear such terms as "Stage keeper" and "House keeper," whose duties may have included the care of properties. Their costs are rarely specified, but a suit by Robert Baden, 12 May 1677, against the King's Company for £135 12s. past due on properties, suggests that the managers invested moderately large sums in supplies.

COSTUMES

More information exists concerning costuming for plays. The agreement between Davenant and his actors, 5 November 1660 (see the section on Management and Operations) attempted to distinguish those articles for which the proprietor was responsible and those which were the personal property of individuals. The agreement specified that Davenant was not obligated to provide from company funds for hats, feathers, gloves, ribbons, sword belts, stockings or shoes (unless these should be specifically required by the playhouse). In 1672, when Mohun, Hart, and Kynaston assisted in the management of the King's Company, the Lord Chamberlain directed, however, that they were to "bee continually furnished" at the charge of the

---

[178] "From Forestage to Proscenium," pp. 13–21.
[179] L. C. 5/138, p. 366, in Thaler, *Shakespere to Sheridan*, p. 290.

Master and the King's Company with specific properties for each: "Two perruques to begin with for the first yeare, One perruque yearely afterwards to begin a yeare hence, Two Cravats yearely, One Lace or point Band in two yeares the first band to be now provided, Three paire of Silke Stockins yearely, Four paire of Shooes yearely, Three Hatts yearely, Two plumes of feathers yearely, Three Shirts with Cuffs to them yearely."[180] In addition, the Crown undertook to supply certain kinds of habits and materials to the players. A warrant dated 29 July 1661 orders the Master of the Great Wardrobe to each of fourteen actors "four yards of Bastard Scarlett for a Cloake and . . . a quarter of a yard of Crimson Velvett for the Cape of itt being the usuall Allowance of every second yeare to commence at October last past."[181] Other kinds of royal assistance occurred with respect to performances in the 1660's, when the playhouses had not fully established themselves or filled their wardrobes. When Davenant staged Love and Honour, 21 October 1661, Downes, the prompter, gave special attention to the fact that the drama was "Richly Cloath'd," for Charles II allowed Betterton to wear the Coronation robes, the Duke of York lent his rich attire to Henry Harris, and Lord Oxford offered his garments to Joseph Price.[182] No doubt, the knowledgeable spectators knew of this loan in advance, and the publicity would have helped to make the affair a gala occasion. These Coronation robes (supplemented with other new habits) were utilized again for Orrery's Henry V at Lincoln's Inn Fields, 13 August 1664. The King also allowed additional sums to the companies for special productions. Pepys, talking with Henry Harris, 11 December 1667, concerning the forthcoming production of Catiline, heard that Charles II had given £500 toward making sixteen scarlet robes for the actors.[183]

With these kinds of assistance and their own resources, the principal companies outfitted a number of new as well as revived plays. According to Downes, when the Duke's Company revived Henry VIII on 22 December 1663, it was "all new Cloath'd in proper Habits: the King's was new, all the Lords, the Cardinals, the Bishops, the Doctors, Proctors, Lawyers, Tip Staves."[184] Count Cominges saw a performance of this play in 1666 and commented upon the habits: "Cardinal Wolsey appears there with his bonnet, and Cranmer, Archbishop of Canterbury, with his rocket and cape,

---

180 L. C. 7/1, in Nicoll, Restoration Drama, p. 365.
181 See Nicoll, Restoration Drama, pp. 363–65, for this order and several subsequent ones.
182 Roscius Anglicanus, p. 21.
183 The production was delayed, however, and it is not certain that the grant ever materialized.
184 Roscius Anglicanus, p. 24.

and even, if I remember aright, his pallium."[185] Among others freshly outfitted were *Mustapha* (3 April 1665), *Heraclius* (8 March 1663/4), *The History
of Charles VIII of France* (18 November 1671), *Macbeth* (18 February 1672/3),
Psyche (27 February 1674/5). No doubt, many other plays were embellished
with new habits, but the principal source of such information, Downes,
prompter to the Duke's Company, naturally emphasized the activities of his
house, and we lack comparable information concerning the King's Company.
That it ordered costumes is indicated by the company's financial difficulties
in the 1670's, for on 5 April 1678 Thomas Jolly sued the King's Company for
£54 for "makeing Cloathes for yᵉ vse of yᵉ Company."[186]

The extent to which costuming conformed to historical accuracy is
uncertain. Allardyce Nicoll, for example, has noted a tendency to use
perriwigs for many characters without regard to realism or anachronism.[187]
A similar failure to outfit the players properly was noted in the criticism
Katherine Philips (see the Calendar, 23 January 1663/4) made of a production
of *Pompey the Great*, for she pointed out that the management had outfitted
the characters in English habits and that "Ceasar was sent in with his
feather & Muff, till he was hiss'd off yᵉ Stage." On the other hand, some
attention was given to authenticity. Pepys attending *Heraclius*, 8 March
1663/4, considered the "garments like Romans very well," and Thomas
Shadwell, writing to Dorset, 19 February 1691/2, emphasized that he
would have a new play, *The Innocent Impostors*, acted "in Roman habits."[188]
And a reference in *The Feast* (Worcester College Plays, 9–22) suggests
that *The Indian Queen* was bedecked with "speckl'd plumes [which] brought
such an Audience."

For some amateur productions at Court, the habits and accoutrement
were very elaborate. The presentation of *Calisto* in the winter of 1674–75
had exceptionally fine staging; Evelyn's account of the jewels worn by
Margaret Blagge, his protégé, and other ladies of quality makes evident
that the principals were richly attired. Many orders for habits also point
to lavish preparations: "twenty garlands" and twenty habits for the
violinists to be "like Indian gownes"; sixty yards of cherry-colored "Avinion";
thirty yards of green; one yard of "sky-coloured"; eighty-four yards of
"silver Gawes"; six yards of "gold gawes"; and four pieces of "Tinsey
Ribon."[189] Eleanore Boswell's full account of all phases of this production

[185] Jusserand, "A French View of England in 1666," p. 794.
[186] Nicoll, *Restoration Drama*, p. 326.
[187] *Ibid.*, pp. 49–50.
[188] *Works*, ed. Montague Summers (London, 1927), I, ccxxix.
[189] Nicoll, *Restoration Drama*, p. 359.

discusses at length the costuming.[190] Obviously this lavish expenditure was beyond the resources of the public theatres, but productions like this one led the theatregoing public, as well as the Court, to a taste for lavish spectacle, fine costumes, and expensive accoutrement.

LIGHTING

Not a great deal is known concerning the details of lighting within the theatres during this period. Candles provided the principal light, and occasional comments suggest that wax candles, more expensive than tallow, had become the vogue. When Killigrew modestly boasted to Pepys concerning the great improvements he had made in his theatre, he emphasized, 12 February 1666/7, that formerly there had been "not above 3 lbs. of tallow" but now "wax-candles, and many of them." The scope of lighting was suggested by Prince Cosmo when he attended *Psyche* at the Duke's Theatre on 24 May 1669, which was "sufficiently lighted on the stage and on the walls to enable the spectators to see the scenes and the performances."[191] No writer of this period has been specific about the nature or dramatic use of lighting, although occasional comments suggest that the age was aware of some of the technical aspects. Certainly the seating area was not darkened during the performance, for the management lacked means of easily controlling the light from candles on the walls and once, as the "Introduction" to *The Damoiselles a la mode* (1667) phrased it, "The Candles lighted before the Curtain's drawn," they were not snuffed out until the play closed. Toward the end of his diary keeping, Pepys constantly refers to the pain in his eyes from the lights of the candles throughout a performance.

On one occasion, however, Pepys noticed an incongruity in the relationship of light to the content of the play and was pleased with his own perceptiveness. Attending *The Heiress* on 2 February 1668/9, he reported: "But it was pleasant to see Beeston come in with others, supposing it to be dark, and yet he is forced to read his part by the light of the candles: and this I observing to a gentleman that sat by me, he was mightily pleased therewith, and spread it up and down." It is possible that sometimes the candles for stage lighting may have been snuffed for scenes requiring a

---

[190] For the costumes, see *Restoration Court Stage*, pp. 214–19; for the entire production, pp. 177–227.

[191] *Travels of Cosmo the Third*, p. 347.

darkened stage, but many practical difficulties stand in the way of frequent use of this mode of relating light to action. In the Prologue to *The Rival Ladies*, Dryden seems to refer to this practice: "They blow out Candles to give Light to th' Plot." Certainly the opening and closing of "scenes" would give an opportunity for the stage hands to snuff and relight candles, but once a "scene" was underway, altering the lights could not be subtly handled.[192]

[192] For a discussion of this problem, see *The Works of John Dryden*, ed. J. H. Smith and Dougald MacMillan (Berkeley, 1962), VIII, 311.

Actors and Acting

IN RESTORATION times acting was in many ways a rewarding profession, for during the first decade after the return of Charles II many actors had close associations with courtiers and the Court, were held in considerable personal esteem by theatregoers, and shared in the stimulating circumstances of helping to revive a professional art which had for many years been eclipsed by official disapproval. Although the salaries for actors were not extremely high, they were satisfactory by comparisons with some occupations requiring little formal education or training, and an actor often had the privilege of becoming a sharer in a company after he had served a period as a hireling or an apprentice. Players in the principal companies also had the status and livery of His Majesty's Company of Comedians and at times had the protection of the Crown.

STATUS

In spite of these advantages, the position of an actor was not particularly secure, and his social position, in spite of favors from gentlemen and the nobility, was a relatively low one. As Sir Ralph Verney, writing in the summer of 1660, stated: "Players and Fiddlers are treated with ignominy by our laws."[193] A player might also be severely punished for taking liberties (especially political license) with his lines, as happened to John Lacy, who, acting the Country Gentleman in *The Change of Crownes*, 15 April 1667, offended Charles II by ad-libbing and was imprisoned, the play also being banned. He might also be in danger of his life, as was William Mountfort, who was murdered on 9–10 December 1692, for defending the honor of Anne Bracegirdle, a performer in his company, his assailants being only lightly punished. He might be so meanly treated by spectators that, like William Smith, an able and experienced actor, he retired from the stage in dismay and anger. An actress was fair game, as was Anne Bracegirdle against her will, or, often willingly, for men of all classes, including the

[193] *Memoirs of the Verney Family*, ed. Margaret M. Verney (London, 1889), IV, 6.

monarch; for men of position, in Downes' inimitable phrase, "erepted" the actresses from the stage. In addition, the professional freedom of the actor was cramped, for he could not easily change companies. When John Richards wished to desert a London company to act in Dublin, the Crown issued a warrant authorizing his arrest and enforced return to London.[194]

GROUPINGS

Although actors, at the resumption of theatrical presentations in 1660, were not classified into rigid categories, several definable groups existed. First of all, a few principals, some possessing experience from pre-Restoration days, became sharers in the companies; frequently ranking among the best actors, they shared in both the professional and financial operations and frequently became leaders of the theatrical community. A prime example is Thomas Betterton, who came to the theatres in 1660 and remained active until 1709. Another category, continuing the Elizabethan practice of boy actors in female roles, consisted of a small group, such as Edward Kynaston, James Nokes, Edward Angel, William Betterton. Pepys emphasized the talents of these impersonators when, on 18 August 1660, he saw *The Loyal Subject*, "where Kinaston, a boy, acted the Duke's sister, but made the loveliest lady that ever I saw in my life, only her voice not very good."

In a short time, however, the theatres abandoned this specialty in favor of women actresses. Uncertainties becloud the time and circumstances of this innovation, and although the first professional actress probably acted in *Othello* on 8 December 1660, her identity has been the subject of much speculation.[195] Soon the actress was a potent member of the repertory company, never to be displaced from it. During the forty years from 1660 to 1700 the theatres introduced several women of unusual histrionic powers, yet the hazards of the profession probably kept from it not only young women of the upper classes but others not so well born. Pepys reported a revealing incident when his friend, Mistress Knepp, who had as her personal maid at the playhouse a charming girl, decided that she must relinquish her services rather than expose her to the pressing attentions of unprincipled young men. The notorious episode of Lord Mohun's pursuit of Anne Bracegirdle, resulting in the death of William

---

[194] *Calendar State Papers Domestic*, 1661–63, p. 455. See also Nicoll, *Restoration Drama*, p. 9n.
[195] For a full discussion of the problem, see Wilson, *All the King's Ladies*, pp. 6–8.

Mountfort, would have frightened a demure young lady from becoming an actress.

A third group of performers had the designation "hirelings." With the development of formally organized companies, the number of sharers was limited, yet a playhouse required a fairly large body of performers and enlisted some on salaries. Although the terms "sharers" and "hirelings" may today suggest a considerable difference in prestige and power, "hireling" had not then a pejorative meaning. A sharer, particularly in the difficult years between 1680 and 1700, might willingly alter his contractual responsibility by going to salary if the change seemed advantageous. Thomas Betterton, for example, occasionally changed from sharer to salaried status and back to sharer, as the structure or prosperity of the company affected his personal welfare. In fact, these arrangements had a considerable flexibility. From 1695 to 1700 in the theatre in Lincoln's Inn Fields the principal actors were whole sharers (without a proprietor) and contracted with others on a salaried basis. As early as 1663–64 Charles Hart, Michael Mohun, and John Lacy became co-managers of Killigrew's Company and displaced sharers, who returned to a salary of £100 yearly;[196] but when this arrangement did not work out well, the salaried actors could be received back as sharers.

Another set of performers, hardly recognizable as a formal classification, were the "young actors," who as apprentices sometimes received privileges that set them apart from the principals. As already pointed out, in the season of 1668–69 the Duke's Company permitted the "young people of the house," as Pepys called them, to have responsibility for reviving John Ford's *The Lady's Trial*, not acted for forty years, on 3 March 1668/9 for their own profit. Two weeks later the young performers revived *The Coxcomb* in similar circumstances. This principle allowed the apprentice to receive pay as well as experience, for during this period apprentices sometimes had to accept a probationary status of three to six months before being admitted to the payroll. Colley Cibber, for example, discussing his entrance into the United Company in 1690, indicated that the patentees "seem'd to make it a Rule that no young Persons desirous to be Actors should be admitted into Pay under at least half a Year's Probation."[197] Later, management allowed the fledgling actors to act, sometimes with the assistance of a few experienced actors, during the summer. In the summer of 1694, for example, the young performers acted on thirty days

---

[196] Hotson, *Commonwealth and Restoration Stage*, p. 245.
[197] *Apology*, I, 181.

for their own benefit, making sufficient profit to sustain them through the Long Vacation.[198] This practice continued into the next century.

RECRUITMENT

Relatively little information exists concerning the recruitment of actors and actresses. In 1660, of course, a few came into the London companies because they had acted in pre-Commonwealth times; among these were Charles Hart and Michael Mohun, who had been apprentices. Edward Kynaston turned to acting after being an apprentice to John Rhodes, the bookseller, and when Rhodes formed a company in 1660, Kynaston started as a boy actor in female roles. Thomas Betterton, possessing a genteel education, seems to have been attracted to the stage by an interest in literature, whereas Cardell Goodman, expelled from Cambridge University, apparently found that the theatre offered a more exciting way of life. William Smith also came from the professions, as he was once a barrister. On the other hand, some actors came from lowly positions. Joseph Williams, trained as a seal cutter, became an apprentice to Henry Harris in the 1670's, and Benjamin Johnson, a sign painter, finding actors an attractive lot, joined an itinerant company and made his way to London. George Powell grew up in the theatres, as his father, Martin Powell, was a member of the King's Company. Colley Cibber typifies the man who came to the stage because the theatre fascinated him: "In my Intervals of Leisure, by frequently seeing Plays, my wise Head was turn'd to higher Views, I saw no Joy in any other Life than that of an Actor . . . 'twas on the Stage alone I had form'd a Happiness preferable to all that Camps or Courts could offer me."[199] Robert Wilks, living in Dublin, acted *Othello* with amateurs and, enthralled, abandoned his other pursuits in favor of acting.

Because the English companies had never had professional actresses, no traditional ways existed by which a young woman could embark upon a theatrical career. Nevertheless, as John Harold Wilson has pointed out in his study of Restoration actresses,[200] the requirements in 1660 were

---

[198] Nicoll, *Restoration Drama*, p. 274.

[199] *Apology*, I, 93. Thomas Davies, *Dramatic Miscellanies* (London, 1784), III, 444, states that Cibber and Verbruggen, dissipated young lads, found the theatre so attractive and so harrassed John Downes, prompter to the United Company, that he eventually let them have apprenticeships.

[200] *All the King's Ladies*, pp. 8–11.

relatively simple—an ability to memorize lines, to speak well, to sing and dance with competence or charm, and attractiveness. The first actresses may have been drawn from the middle classes pretty much by chance. As actresses secured a firm position in the theatrical organization, later ones came in by choice and apprenticeship rather than by the circumstance of availability when the companies opened their arms to women performers. Elizabeth Barry, for example, came to the attention of Lord Rochester, who coached her in elocution and introduced her to the managers. Anne Bracegirdle apparently began as a child performer, speaking prologues and epilogues and playing children's roles, graduating to maturer parts. Susanna Percival got her opportunity because she was the daughter of a minor actor, Thomas Percival. Nell Gwyn began as an orangewoman in the King's Company, became the mistress of Charles Hart, a foremost actor in the same company. Similarly, Anne Reeves may have owed her short career to her being the reputed mistress of John Dryden, the principal playwright in the King's Company. Perhaps some actresses, like the actor Joseph Haines, gained their experience in the Nurseries, but no example as certain as his can be cited.

A performer entered a company of moderate size in which versatility as well as a degree of specialization was necessary and admired. Although we lack accurate statistics concerning the rosters of the companies, the number of players usually did not exceed twenty-five or thirty. When Killigrew and Davenant briefly ruled a United Company in the autumn of 1660, the actors numbered about twenty; later that winter, when the companies divided, Killigrew's numbered at least thirteen.[201] The rosters of the companies at the beginning of each season in the Calendar suggest also that the number of men was ordinarily at least twice as great as the number of women, a proportion extending roughly into the next century. The most detailed list of players specifically dated is a document in the Kent Archives Office, 20 July 1695.[202] For the company in Lincoln's Inn Fields it lists fifteen male actors, "and Severall new taken in"; eleven actresses and "Severall New taken in," as well as "A fine Danceing Girle"; the prompter, two dancers, and three singers (one a woman). For the company at Drury Lane the list names eleven actors "And Several New taken in"; eight women "And Several new taken in," but does not specify the other personnel. A glance at the texts of Restoration plays will show that the number of male roles usually ran two to three times the number

201 Nicoll, *Restoration Drama*, pp. 293–94.
202 Rosenfeld, "Unpublished Stage Documents," p. 94.

of female characters.²⁰³ The proportion of the sexes in singing and dancing roles, however, is more nearly equal.

CONTRACTS

As has already been pointed out, the performers, no matter their status or specialty, were hedged in by restrictions, although the sharers, naturally, had more power within the company. Being contracted to a single company and sworn in as one of His Majesty's Comedians, a performer had little freedom of contract. He might, however, leave London and try the provinces, as Cardell Goodman, James Gray, and Thomas Clarke did in 1679, when the affairs of the King's Company were precarious; or, like John Perin, he might play in the provinces occasionally (Perin acted in Norwich), in London during some seasons. In the last decade of the century the enterprising Dublin companies attracted several players, such as Benjamin Husband, William Penkethman, Richard Leveridge, and Robert Wilks, who sometimes had a season in Dublin or London as a variation from their regular appointments. On the other hand, if he remained in London, he might well be coerced into holding his situation. When Henry Harris, in the summer of 1663 (see the Calendar, 22 July 1663) attempted to change companies, the King intervened and ordered him to remain with his contract. In addition, a player might be removed from a role by royal preference, as happened to Walter Clun, who, according to Pepys, 8 May 1663, was ousted from playing the Lieutenant in *The Humorous Lieutenant* and, at the King's command, replaced by John Lacy. Nevertheless, a player had a right to appeal a decision. In May 1667 Anne Quin of the King's Company had quarreled with the management because another actress had usurped her parts; she left the company and petitioned the Lord Chamberlain, who ordered her reinstatement.²⁰⁴ On the other hand, a player might well have no recourse when a segment of the audience turned against him. A classic case, in which even the favor of the King was of no avail, is William Smith's withdrawal from the stage. As Cibber stated:

Even when a Royal Resentment has shewn itself in the behalf of an injur'd Actor, it has been unable to defend him from farther Insults! an Instance of which

---

²⁰³ In two of Orrery's plays, for example, *Henry V* required 14 actors, 4 actresses; *Mustapha* specified 10 male parts, 5 female.

²⁰⁴ L. C. 5/138, p. 376, in Nicoll, *Restoration Drama*, p, 321n.

happen'd in the late King James's time. Mr Smith (whose Character as a Gentleman could have been no way impeach'd had he not degraded it by being a celebrated Actor) had the Misfortune, in a Dispute with a Gentleman behind the Scenes, to receive a Blow from him: The same Night an Account of this Action was carry'd to the King, to whom the Gentleman was represented so grossly in the wrong, that the next Day his Majesty sent to forbid him the Court upon it. This Indignity cast upon a Gentleman only for having maltreated a Player, was look'd upon as the Concern of every Gentleman: and a Party was soon form'd to assert and vindicate their Honour, by humbling this favour'd Actor, whose slight Injury had been judg'd equal to so severe a Notice. Accordingly, the next time Smith acted he was receiv'd with a Chorus of Cat-calls, that soon convinc'd him he should not be suffer'd to proceed in his Part; upon which, without the least Discompasure, he order'd the Curtain to be dropp'd; and, having a competent Fortune of his own, thought the Conditions of adding to it by his remaining upon the Stage were too dear, and from that Day entirely quitted it.[205]

For the early years following the Restoration, the evidence does not make fully clear the contractual relationships of an actor to his company so far as salaries and working conditions were concerned. For the sharers, this usually was not a major issue, for they participated in the profits, and the benefit as a formal part of the actor's contract had not yet genuinely materialized. Although the companies occasionally issued directives concerning the use of costumes and properties, until the theatres declined in prosperity and joined in 1682, formal contracts apparently were brief, pertaining principally to salaries.[206] After the United Company dissolved in 1695, either management and performers spelled out their relationships more fully or more examples of contracts have survived. A few documents indicate the basic provisions prepared by Sir Thomas Skipwith and Christopher Rich. On 3 April 1696, for example, Thomas Dogget contracted for a salary of £4 for each unit of six acting days (or more, if George Powell or John Verbruggen received more), with a benefit of an old play acted on a Wednesday or Friday in Lent, Dogget to pay the charges of the house. Further, Dogget was to act nowhere else, and both parties were to give bond.[207] A less comprehensive contract for William Bullock, 15 April 1695, specified that he was to act only with Rich's company at a salary of 20s. weekly, the contract to be terminated

[205] Apology, I, 78–79.

[206] An informal pension system existed. When Philip Cademan was injured on stage in the summer of 1673, the company gave him a pension of 30s. weekly and others disabled by sickness or misfortune had similar gratuities. In the 1690's, when Christopher Rich became proprietor, he cut off Cademan's pension entirely when the latter could not do simple tasks such as collect tickets. See Nicoll, Restoration Drama, pp. 367–68.

[207] Ibid., p. 383.

only on nine months' notice.208 In 1694–95 Elizabeth Barry had a very liberal agreement, a salary of 50s. weekly, with a benefit every year. Later her arrangement with Betterton specified that if her benefit did not equal £70, augmentation by the company must bring her net benefit to that figure.209 A variety of documents make evident that dissension often arose over salaries and working conditions; the controversy between Betterton (as representative of the dissenting actors), on the one hand, and the Patentees of the United Company, on the other hand, before Betterton broke away in 1694–95 illustrates in detail the accumulated grievances which, contract or no contract, destroyed the harmony of the company.210

SALARIES

The lack of Restoration account books makes impossible a systematic discussion of the salary ranges. Basically, an apprentice, especially in the years Cibber reports on, came in at no salary for three to six months, perhaps longer. Although Cibber reported that he found his payless apprenticeship a joyous period, if only because he welcomed the opportunity to see all the plays free of charge, he eventually, after three quarters of a year, went onto the rolls at ten shillings weekly. When the company dissolved in 1694–95, Cibber stayed with the Patentees, who, desperately seeking a full complement of actors, raised him to 30s.211 Thomas Dogget moved somewhat rapidly from an opening salary of 10s. weekly in 1690, after experience as a stroller, to articles allowing him 40s. weekly and nine months' notice in February 1693. Later he rose to 50s. weekly, very close to the maximum stipend at the end of the century.212

STANDARDS OF PERFORMING

In return for his share or salary, the management and the town expected excellence in performance and a sufficient versatility to play several types of characters, perhaps to sing and dance, certainly to speak prologues and epilogues, to keep in his memory an extremely large number of roles—during

208 *Ibid.*, p. 384.
209 *Ibid.*, p. 369.
210 *Ibid.*, pp. 368–69.
211 *Apology*, I, 181, 194.
212 Nicoll, *Restoration Drama*, p. 378.

the forty years from 1660 to 1700 Betterton played in 132 named roles and was in at least nine other plays—and constantly to learn new roles and refresh himself in old ones. The repertory system made great demands upon actors, for the frequent (sometimes daily) change of play and the preparation of new and newly revived dramas called for constant study and rehearsals. Perhaps no theatrical system put such constant demands upon the talents and powers of an actor as the repertory arrangements of the seventeenth and eighteenth centuries, yet the variety of opportunities and duties produced extremely able and versatile performers. Under these circumstances, the players could not always please the audience or the dramatist, and diaries and prefaces to plays indicate some of the deficiencies in acting. As a spectator Pepys is our best authority for certain kinds of defects which disturbed him. He sincerely believed, for example, that Nell Gwyn's talents lay in comedy, songs, and dance, and he praised highly her comic portrayals, yet he was distressed to see her attempt, either by her own choice or by persuasion of the management, a tragic role. He was "infinitely displeased with her being put to act the Emperour's daughter, which is a great and serious part, which she do most basely" (*The Indian Emperour*, 22 August 1667). At a repetition of the play on 11 November 1667, he held the same view: "above all things Nell's ill speaking of a great part made me mad."

Another weakness frequently emphasized was imperfect retention of lines. This defect appeared most noticeably and naturally at premières, when the actors often had insufficient time to perfect themselves. Nevertheless, the audience did not make exceptions for inadequacy in recitation. The première of Etherege's *She Would if She Could* was a partial disappointment because of an imperfect representation. Pepys alluded to this weakness, and Shadwell, some years later, remembered it well enough to cite it in the Preface to *The Humorists* as a cause of permanent damage to the reputation of the play. Shadwell felt also that the failure of the actors was a cause of a poor reception for *The Humorists*. Similarly, Edward Howard, in the Preface to *The Women's Conquest* (ca. November 1670) complained that some roles were "ill and imperfectly performed." At *The Bondman* (28 July 1664), a play Pepys usually admired, Pepys could not avoid commenting upon the fact that "for want of practice they had many of them forgot their parts a little."

Defects of this kind were understandable in the confusion of rehearsals and revivals, but other weaknesses were regarded as more blameable. Pepys felt disgust when the actors stepped out of character or did not exert their best powers. On consecutive days, 4 and 5 September 1667, he found the Duke's players insufficiently disciplining themselves. On the first day, at

Mustapha, he disliked the fact that both "Betterton and Harris could not refrain from laughing in the midst of a most serious part, from the ridiculous mistake of one of the men upon the stage, which I did not like." On the following day, at *Heraclius*, he complained that the actors "did so spoil it with their laughing, and being all of them out, and with the noises they made within the theatre, that I was ashamed of it." In contrast, Cibber complimented Mountfort for his self-discipline: "He never laugh'd at his own Jest, unless the Point of his Raillery upon another requir'd it.—He had a particular talent in giving life to bon mots and Repartees: The Wit of the Poet seem'd always to come from him extempore."[213] Inattentiveness of another kind drew Pepys' disapproval on 10 June 1663 at *The Changes*. Admiring Lacy in a role, Pepys added, "but for the rest which are counted such old and excellent actors, in my life I never heard both men and women so ill pronounce their parts, even to my making myself sick therewith." Essentially Pepys directed his criticism at the failure of professional actors always to perform at their most disciplined best.

A somewhat different order of professional responsibility concerned fidelity to the author's words. Ad-libbing sometimes had serious consequences, such as the example already cited of John Lacy's punishment for expanding his lines in *The Change of Crownes* on 15 April 1667 when he acted before the King. Later, in the Preface to *The Dutch Lover*, 6 February 1672/3, Aphra Behn complained bitterly of the liberties Edward Angel took with her play, how he had introduced extensive passages which she had never before heard and which, in her judgment, did irreparable harm to her reputation. Another form of irresponsibility was an imperfect representation resulting from a lack of sobriety. The author of *The Wary Widow*, ca. March 1692/3, in the Preface painted a picture of a cast so lost in drink that the play was eclipsed by the misdemeanors of the actors. And a memorable evening for the spectators was the première of *The Relapse*, 21 November 1696, when Verbruggen, acting Loveless, had imbibed so freely before the play as well as in onstage drinking scenes that he was on the verge of assaulting Mrs Rogers in actuality instead of doing so only vicariously.

With almost no formal reviewing of plays and with limited comments in diaries, correspondence, and prefaces, it is difficult to determine acutely the expectation of the audience as to proper professional acting standards. Pepys is, of course, the most satisfactory spectator whose observations we know in detail, for he enjoyed the theatre and he reacted in particular as well as general terms. He clearly expected, though not to an unreasonable

[213] *Apology*, I, 128.

degree, perfection in lines, proper casting for each role, consistency in character portrayal, and good rapport between spectator and actor. As a generalization he summed up his preferences on 13 January 1664/5: "being ill-satisfied with the present actings of the [King's] House, and prefer the other House [Duke's] before this infinitely." Furthermore, when he admired an actor, he did so genuinely. He rarely attended a performance of *The Bondman* with Betterton in the title role without expressing superlative pleasure, and his early enthusiasm was evident on 20 November 1660 when he saw Michael Mohun in *The Beggar's Bush* and called him "the best actor in the world."

SPECIALIZATION

Finally, the actors of this period, like those of many ages, could not help specializing. Betterton, for example, was at his best in heroic and tragic roles, although he played well some roles in high comedy (in Congreve's comedies, for example). Charles Hart especially well portrayed princes and kings, and Downes recorded the statement of a contemporary that Hart could well "Teach any King on Earth how to comport himself."[214] John Lacy and Joseph Haines excelled in the rougher, less subtle comic roles. Samuel Sandford often portrayed villains, although his specialization may not have been so extreme as tradition has implied.[215] Joseph Haines became an inimitable speaker of prologues and epilogues and developed some techniques (such as an Epilogue Spoken upon an Ass) which Thomas Dogget and William Penkethman, to name only two, imitated in the next century. Among the actresses Nell Gwyn excelled in comic rather than tragic roles, whereas Elizabeth Barry made a greater name in tragic and heroic roles. Anne Bracegirdle was a superlative actress in high comedy. As a result of these special qualifications, many dramatists wrote with particular performers in mind. Thomas Otway, for example, created Malagene in *Friendship in Fashion* for Anthony Leigh. William Congreve created his most gracious heroines with Anne Bracegirdle as a model. With other examples in mind, John Dennis, developing some broad generalizations, wrote in 1711 that this characteristic of Restoration playwrights may have been excessively developed.

   For it has been a Complaint of Two Thousand Years standing, that Poets have been us'd to violate their Subjects, and to force their Characters out of complaisance

---

[214] *Roscius Anglicanus*, p. 16.
[215] See Robert H. Ross Jr, "Samuel Sandford: Villain from Necessity," *PMLA*, LXXVI (1961), 367–72.

to their Actors, that is, to their Interest. Most of the Writers for the Stage in my time, have not only adapted their Characters to their Actors, but those actors have as it were sate for them. For which reason the Lustre of the most Shining of their Characters must decay with the Actors.[216]

---

[216] *Reflections Critical and Satyrical*, in *Works*, I, 418.

Dancers and Dancing

AFTER 1660 the relatively steady growth of entr'acte entertainments as well as those within the acts of the play created a greater emphasis upon dancing, instrumental and vocal music, and upon performers possessing skills in both acting and specialties. Although some actors, like Betterton, concentrated their talents upon performing, others, like Nell Gwyn, developed a series of specialties and could act, sing, dance, and, sometimes, play musical instruments. Similarly, the development of the conception that an afternoon at the theatre involved not only a play but a spectrum of entertainments created sufficient differences among the specialties that each type will be discussed separately. In the general realm of choreography are the ballet, the dance integral to the play, the dance between the act, and rope dancing. The ballet (which will be discussed later in the section on The Repertory: Specialties) and rope dancing, widely diverse forms, were most frequently seen at Court and at the Fairs, less frequently within the professional theatres. In fact, the lowest form on the artistic scale was rope dancing, essentially a demonstration of dexterity by a skilled performer who combined dancing with rope skipping and rope twirling. In spite of its great contrast with the ballet and masque, it had, apparently, an equal following at Court and at the Fairs. Rope dancers, for example, performed at Whitehall in August 1660, again on 25 October 1667, and in the Banquetting Hall on 19 September 1671.[217] The extant records offer scanty information concerning these performances. For similar entertainments the lower classes (sometimes the nobility, incognito, as well) attended Bartholomew and Southwark Fairs, where the most famous rope dancer was Jacob Hall, a performer whose dexterities Pepys occasionally witnessed and with whom he sometimes chatted concerning the characteristics of his art. At the end of the century there came into vogue the diversified dancer, who performed on the slanting rope, over and through obstacles, creating intricate patterns. This form of entertainment also continued to be popular in the next century.

Far more significant for theatrical dancing were the dances within plays and between the acts, whether related or unrelated to the atmosphere of the

[217] Boswell, *Restoration Court Stage*, p. 25, and *The Bulstrode Papers*, I, 4.

drama performed. Soon after the opening of the theatres the dance became an integral part of many plays, especially those of an operatic or spectacular nature. In the season of 1662–63 Pepys, for example, commented occasionally upon the vogue for dances. On 29 September 1662 he saw the King's Company intersperse dances among the scenes of *A Midsummer Night's Dream*. At the first performance of Tom Porter's *The Villain*, 18 October 1662, dances were emphasized, and Pepys saw them on the third performance. At Drury Lane on 8 May 1663 at *The Humorous Lieutenant* he thought that "in the dance, the tall devil's Actions was very pretty." These entertainments were of a great diversity. In *The Royal Shepherdess* on 25 February 1668/9 in Act II was a "Dance with Gittars and Castaniettas." In the same play Pepys found "nothing pleasing . . . but a good martial dance of pikemen, where Harris and another do handle their pikes in a dance to admiration." In Act III of *The Town Fop* was a "Jigg" and in Act V of *The Old Troop* Lacy performed "a Jig." In *The Indian Queen* (Act III), 25 January 1663/4, "The Indians . . . advance in a warlike Dance." In Act III of Mrs Behn's *Sir Patient Fancy* is a "Rustick Antick." In *The Black Prince* on 1 April 1668 Pepys found, appropriately, "the dance very stately." All of these played a functional role in the play, either as entertainments given before the characters in the drama, or as contributory to the atmosphere. In the more elaborate spectacles these embellishments played a larger role. In *The Tempest*, 1674, Act V has a "Dance of twelve Tritons," the Second Epilogue adding, "And we have Singing, Dancing Devills here." More detailed examples appear in the text of *Psyche*, 27 February 1674/5. In Act I is an "Entry by Four Sylvans and Four Dryads to Rustick Musick." In Act II: "A Dance of Priests entrying from each side of the Stage, with Cymbals, Bells, and Flambeaux." In Act III: "A Cyclops Dance." It is this union of drama and embellishment which led Pepys to speak of *Love's Mistress*, 15 August 1668, as being "full of variety of divertisement."

The dance served another theatrical function: a part of the entr'acte entertainment. In fact, this alteration of the nature of the program, which became strongly accentuated in the next century, is a contribution of the late seventeenth century to the theory that the spectators are to be entertained during their three hours in the theatre. Many statements in prologues, epilogues, and the text of plays indicate that the intervals between acts allowed an opportunity for social chat, flirtations, and occasionally unruly behavior; the presentation of entr'acte entertainment, though not universally practiced in the first decades after the reopening of the theatres, may have contributed to a better decorum within the theatre. Certainly, many of these dances had little relationship, in theme or substance, to the play. At the first performance of *The Sullen Lovers*, 2 May 1668, Pepys greatly enjoyed a dance which apparently had no integral relationship to the play: "But a little boy, for a farce, do dance Polichinelle, the best that ever anything was done in the world, by all men's report." Certainly this was true of the entertainments at *Horace*, a tragedy, acted on 16 January 1668/9. Mrs John Evelyn, summarizing the performance, described the program as having "a farce and dances between every act, composed by Lacy and played by him and Nell [Gwyn], which takes." Pepys, writing on 19 January 1668/9, clarified the nature of one element in the entertainment: "but Lacy had made a farce of several dances—between each act, one: but his words are but silly, and invention not extraordinary, as to the dances; only some Dutchmen come out of the mouth and tail of a Hamburgh sow." This "farce" obviously had little thematic relationship to a tragedy. Some of the appeal of the dances lay in costuming and particularity. Pepys described as "admirable" a dance at the end of *The Sea Voyage*, 25 September 1667, "of the ladies, in a military manner." Women dancing in men's habits were very taking. At *The English Princess* on 7 March 1666/7 Pepys enjoyed "little Mis. Davis [dancing] a jig . . . only to please the company to see her dance in boy's clothes," just as Nell Gwyn's appearance in man's attire a few days earlier had caught his eye. At *Hamlet*, 2 December 1674, there was dancing between the acts. At Tate's *The Ingratitude of a Commonwealth*, 14 January 1681/2, a commentator reported: "with dancing and volting." By the end of the century the occasional theatrical advertisements make abundantly clear the prevalence of entr'acte entertainments.

In spite of the greater emphasis upon dancing, the members of companies who concentrated upon that specialty are not fully known. We do know of Josias Priest, Luke Channell, John Dowson (who was entertained in the King's Company on 10 December 1680 but who did not enter into articles), Monsieur l'Abbe, Mr Bray, Monsieur St Andre, Monsieur Balon, and, of course, others who like John Lacy, Joseph Haines, Nell Gwyn, and Mrs Johnson danced as well as acted. Occasionally the management engaged a corps of dancers. John Lacy, for example, stated that he had made an agreement with Louis Grabut that French dancing masters would perform for the King's Company at ten shillings each day they performed,[218] and on another occasion Killigrew, Hart, and Lacy agreed to engage six dancers for five shillings daily whether they performed or not.

Toward the end of the century more documentation exists concerning the frequency of entr'acte entertainments. On 8 April 1699 Monsieur Balon,

[218] L. C. 5/140, p. 472, in Nicoll, *Restoration Drama*, p. 60.

a celebrated dancing master, had leave to perform in London for five weeks at the extraordinary sum of 400 guineas,[219] a reward far exceeding the fondest hopes of a contemporary actor. During the seasons of 1698–99 and 1699–1700 the bills or editions of plays indicate a variety of dances. At *The Pilgrim* on 6 July 1700 Weaver, Cottin, and Miss Campion danced in the intervals an *Entry* composed by the late Eaglesfield; during another interval the audience saw a dance by a Bonny Highlander. At Lincoln's Inn Fields on 5 July 1700 at *Don Quixote*, the bill named two entr'acte turns: a jig and an Irish dance.

To no one's surprise, the vogue of entr'acte show brought numerous jibes. In Shadwell's *The Sullen Lovers*, 1668, Act II, a character ridicules the love of the audience for spectacle and excitement: "At t'other house there's a rare Play, with a Jigg in it . . . but if there were nothing else in't, you might have your four shillings out in Thunder and Lightning." The Preface satirized spectators for looking "big upon the success of an ill Play, stuff'd full of Songs and Dances . . . when in such Playes the Composer and the Danceing-Master are the best Poets." In Otway's *Friendship in Fashion*, Malagene (written for Thomas Jevon, who was once a dancing-master) declares: "I'm a very good mimick; I can act Punchinello, Scaramuchio, Harlequin, Prince Prettyman, or any thing." In the Prologue to Edward Howard's *The Women's Conquest*, 1671, the speaker declares: "We are to act a farce to-day that has sixteen Mimics in it . . . with two and thirty Dances and Jiggs a la mode." The Prologue to *Every Man Out of His Humour*, July 1675, ridicules the love for the French dancers.

> The most Nymphs now ev'ry heart will win,
> With the surprising ways of Harlequin.
> . . . .
>
> While you Gallants—
> Who for dear Missie ne'r can do to much,
> Make Courtships alamode de Scarramouch.

At the end of the century the same attitude, part lament, part indignation, part enjoyment, prevailed. Tom Brown, writing on 12 September 1699 and comparing the theatres with Bartholomew Fair, stated: "Poetry is so little regarded there [at the playhouses], and the Audience is so taken up with show and sight, that an Author need not much Trouble himself about his Thoughts and Languages, so he is in Fee with the Dancing-Masters, and

[219] Luttrell, *A Brief Relation*, I, 502–3.

has but a few luscious Songs to Lard his dry Composition."[220] In the same year the author of *Historia Histrionica* summed up the view of the high-minded who disapproved the mixed program: "It is an Argument of the Worth of the Plays and Actors, of the last Age, and easily inferr'd, that they were much beyond ours in this, to consider that they cou'd support them-selves meerly from their own merit; the weight of the Matter, and goodness of the Action, without Scenes and Machines. Whereas the present Plays with all that shew, can hardly draw an Audience, unless there be the addi-tional Invitation of a Signior Fidelia, a Monsieur L'Abbe, or some such Foreign Regale exprest at the bottom of the Bill."[221]

To modern students of the theatre, however, these laments should be partially looked upon as an insistence that the playhouse should be restricted to the drama alone, a conception which the English theatre had steadily altered in the light of a desire for change, for variety, for embellishment. Not all of these innovations obviously were of equal merit, but the concept of variety in the midst of the traditional, of experimentation in the midst of the preservation of the best from the past, or the new with the old was the century's way of trying to establish a vitally live theatre.

[220] *Works*, 4th. ed. (London, 1715), I, 216.
[221] In Cibber, *Apology*, I, xxvii–xxviii.

Musicians, Singers, and Music

ONE of the striking phenomena of the world of entertainment between 1660 and 1700 is the steadily growing vogue of music at Court, in the theatres, and especially in the concert halls. Although all of these modes of musical presentation had existed earlier, with the exception of the concert hall, the popularity of instrumental and vocal music as an integral part of plays, as entr'acte entertainments, and as concerts (weekly, sometimes daily) foreshadows the still greater preoccupation of the next century with music, when the Italian opera and the creation of the Royal Academy of Music greatly strengthened the role of music in London cultural life. Immediately following the restoration of Charles II, indications of the role that music was to play in the next forty years made themselves evident. As early as 1660 Charles II by a grant to Giulio Gentileschi on 22 October 1660 to bring Italian opera to London expressed an interest in this novelty although nothing came of the proposal at the moment. Thomas Killigrew, talking with Pepys on 2 August 1664, enthusiastically planned to build a Nursery in Moorfields, where, in addition to offering plays, he intended to stage four operas each season, each to have a run of six weeks. To implement this program, he proposed importing singers from Italy. Although nothing materialized immediately from this scheme, Italian singers arrived and became popular figures among Englishmen. On 12 February 1666/7, for example, Pepys attended a concert where he heard Giovanni Baptista Draghi sing. In addition, he learned that Draghi had "composed a play in Italian for the Opera, which T. Killigrew do intend to have up, and here he did sing one of the acts." The influence of Italian music shows in an occasional entry, such as the statement in Act III of Mrs Behn's *The City Heiress*: "Here is an Italian Song in two Parts."

INSTRUMENTAL

At the same time that these foreign influences stirred an interest in music, the theatres and Court inherited a tradition of songs and instrumental accompaniments or concerts from the Elizabethan age. For many decades lyrics had served functional as well as decorative functions in plays, and in the age of Shakespeare songs had become an integral part of comedies and tragedies.[222] Instrumental music as a solo or orchestral accompaniment to the daily program had also established itself. When the new theatre in Bridges Street opened on 8 May 1663, Pepys, keenly interested in music, gave special attention to the orchestra, finding it rather poorly placed, so that he was not certain that the trebles and basses could be equally well heard. The orchestra performed several functions. First of all, it entertained the audience with overtures before the play began. Writing in 1664, Samuel de Sorbière stated: "The Musick with which you are entertained diverts your time till the Play begins, and People chuse to go in betimes to hear it."[223] A stage direction in Shadwell's *The Tempest* (1674) in Act I specifies "While the Overture is playing," and in Shadwell's *A True Widow*, ca. December 1678, a scene (Act IV) set in a playhouse refers to the orchestra: "They play the Curtain-time." The popularity of orchestral music was emphasized in a Prologue to *Volpone* (ca. 17 January 1675/6) on an occasion when "a Consort of Hautboyes were added to the Musick."

> *Did Ben now live, how would he fret, and rage,*
> *To see the Musick-room envye the stage?*
> *To see the French Haut-boyes charm the listning Pitt*
> *More than the Raptures of his God-like wit!*
>
> . . . .
>
> *Musick, which was by Intervals design'd*
> *To ease the weary'd Actors voice and mind,*
> *You to the Play judiciously prefer,*
> *'Tis now the bus'ness of the Theatre.*[224]

During the play the orchestra as well as an occasional solo instrument performed several functions. The musicians played concerts or solos within the acts, accompanied the vocalists, and created background music to heighten the atmosphere. In Act IV of Shadwell's *The Royal Shepherdess*, 25 February 1668/9, following a "Sacrifice . . . There is a Consort of Martial

[222] For an extensive list of studies of music in Elizabethan plays, see R. G. Noyes, "Conventions of Song in Restoration Tragedy," *PMLA*, LIII (1938), 162-63.

[223] As translated in *A Voyage to England*, p. 71. In *The Travels of Prince Cosmo* (15 April 1669, p. 191) much the same point is made: "Before the comedy begins, that the audience may not be tired with waiting, the most delightful symphonies are played; on which account many persons come early to enjoy this agreeable amusement."

[224] R. G. Noyes, "A Manuscript Restoration Prologue for *Volpone*," *Modern Language Notes*, XLII (1937), pp. 198-200.

Musick." In fact, numerous entries in the texts of plays specify "The Musick Plays," either as an entertainment for a character or "scene" on stage or to fill in while the action is momentarily suspended, as in "Then in the second Act, with a Flourish of the Fiddles, I change the Scene."[225] The elaborate accompaniments for songs appear in the stage directions for Act I of *The Tempest* (1674): "The Front of the Stage is open'd, and the Band of 24 Violins, with the Harpsicals and Theorbo's, which accompany the Voices, are plac'd between the Pit and the Stage." As for atmospheric music, two examples will show the extremes. At *The Virgin Martyr*, 27 February 1667/8, Pepys was enraptured by one refrain: "But that which did please me beyond any thing in the whole world was the wind-musique when the angel comes down, which is so sweet that it ravished me, and indeed, in a word, did wrap up my soul so that it made me really sick, just as I have formerly been when in love with my wife." In contrast, a passage in Shadwell's *The Sullen Lovers*, 2 May 1668, ridicules some of the effects: "Their Tooting Instruments make a more Hellish Noise than they do at a Playhouse, when they flourish for the Entrance of the Witches." At the end of the century the author of *Historia Histrionica* (1699) generalized upon the quality of the orchestra since 1660: "All this while the Play-house Musick Improved Yearly; and is now arrived to greater Perfection than ever I knew it."[226]

The size of the orchestra is not certain; in fact, it may have varied a good deal according to the needs of the program. Samuel Chappuzeau, writing in 1667,[227] referred to twelve violins in the London theatres, a statement which corresponds fairly well to Killigrew's reference on 12 February 1666/7, speaking to Pepys, to nine or ten fiddlers as the number desired in his projected theatre. The stage directions for *The Tempest*, as already noted, call for twenty-four violins, possibly a special augmentation for an operatic work, yet on 18 February 1678/9, for plays acted at Court, the Lord Chamberlain ordered Nicholas Staggins to have twenty-four violins attend every Court play.[228] The stage directions refer also to a variety of instruments: in Act I of *Psyche*, 27 February 1674/5: "Flajolets, Violins, Cornets, Sackbuts, Hoa-boys." Nevertheless, the greatest emphasis is upon the violins. The extant records refer occasionally to other aspects of the orchestra. As to pay, Davenant's original agreement with the actor-sharers call for "a Consort of Musiciens" to be paid thirty shillings daily out of

[225] G. Farquhar, *A Discourse Upon Comedy, Works*, I, 104.
[226] In Cibber's *Apology*, I, xxxii.
[227] See Nicoll, *Restoration Drama*, p. 62n.
[228] L. C. 5/142, p. 272, in Boswell, *Restoration Court Stage*, p. 99.

general receipts.[229] Sometimes the musicians were specially garbed; for example, an order of the Lord Chamberlain, 25 January 1663/4,[230] provided Thomas Killigrew with £40 to clothe the musicians for a performance on that date of *The Indian Queen*. In addition, orders treat the customary complaints: that they absented themselves without leave from rehearsal or that they failed to observe proper decorum when they performed in the theatre without removing their hats.

VOCAL

From the pre-Commonwealth era the theatres inherited lyric embellishment for plays, both tragedies and comedies. For tragedy R. G. Noyes has copiously illustrated the functions of songs, and most of his principles apply equally well to comedy.[231] He points out that, in principle though not always in practice, the writers of tragedy "wove lyrics into the fabric of their plays with great discretion, if not always with great originality." The song served, for example, the useful function of opening the play, and Noyes offers an illustration from Lee's *The Princess of Cleve*, when the Duke of Nemours, entering, hears the fiddles playing at the drawing of the curtain and speaks: "Hold you there Monsieur Devol; prithe leave off playing fine in Consort. . . . So now the Song, call in the Eunuch; come my pretty Stallion, Hem and begin." Another useful convention called for singing to a character asleep at the opening of the curtain. Similarly, a song (as did instrumental music) could define the episodes within a scene or create the illusion of the passage of time. Songs also served to heighten characterization, to strengthen the emotional intensity of a scene, or to create an atmosphere, perhaps of love, death, or foreboding. For plays employing a procession—martial, religious, nuptial, sacrificial—songs served thematically to develop the mood and to give order to the mass of characters on stage. During the period from 1660 to 1700 a large proportion of the plays, both comic and tragic, had at least one song, and as the vogue of theatrical singing increased, older plays, newly revived, often had additional songs composed for the revivals. In Otway's *Friendship in Fashion*, ca. April 1678, Saunter, commenting upon a new tragedy, states: "I did not like it neither for my part; there was never a song in it." In addition to the plays which had a few songs, whether

[229] Herbert, *Dramatic Records*, pp. 96–100.
[230] L. C. 5/138, in Nicoll, *Restoration Drama*, p. 354.
[231] "Conventions of Song in Restoration Tragedy," pp, 162–88.

introduced thematically or incidentally, the development of the musical drama and the operatic work vastly increased the number of songs, for a work like *Bonduca*, *The World in the Moon*, *King Arthur*, *The Grove*, or *The Island Princess* called for song after song.

During this period the song as an entr'acte entertainment was not so firmly established as instrumental music between the acts, but the growing emphasis upon almost continuous entertainment from the raising of the curtain to the end of the program opened the way for more and more songs, old and new. Obviously, most of these do not appear in the text of plays, and it is only toward the end of the century when the playbills began to list the entr'acte entertainments that considerable evidence appears. Nevertheless, Noyes cites some examples of tragedies in which the text calls for songs between the acts. Just before Act II of *Aureng-Zebe* the stage directions state: "Betwixt the Acts, a Warlike Tune is plaid." More specific evidence appears in Katherine Philips' *Pompey* (1663), which has five heroic "Songs between the Acts, which were added only to lengthen the Play, and make it fitter for the Stage." Lee's *Theodosius* also has inter-act songs in the text.[232] So few complete bills exist before 1700 that only sketchy examples of entr'acte songs appear in them, such as "a new Pastoral Dialogue" at a performance of *Don Quixote* on 5 July 1700 and a "Scotch Song" accompanying the "Dance of the Bonny Highlander" at *The Pilgrim* on 6 July 1700.

The vast number of songs in the context of plays, in entr'acte offerings, and in the concert halls may be most easily comprehended by examining the compilation by C. L. Day and Eleanore Boswell Murrie, in which thousands of songs are listed.[233] Many of these, after appearing in plays, were reprinted in the numerous anthologies published between 1680 and 1700, the music sometimes being reprinted and the composer and singer being named. The appeal to the spectator shows most clearly in Pepys' response, for his interest in music made him curious concerning the origin, composition, theory, and effect of a song. His pleasure showed in his attendance at *The Tempest*, 7 November 1667: "and a curious piece of musique in an echo of half sentences, the echoe repeating the former half, while the man goes on to the latter, which is mighty pretty." He found this work so attractive that

[232] *Ibid.*, p. 168.

[233] *English Song-Books, 1651–1702*. See also three articles by R. G. Noyes, "Contemporary Musical Settings of the Songs in Restoration Dramatic Operas," *Harvard Studies and Notes in Philology and Literature*, XX (1938), 99–121; "Songs from Restoration Drama in Contemporary and Eighteenth Century Poetical Miscellanies," *ELH*, III (1946), 291–316; "Broadside-Balled Versions of the Songs in Restoration Drama" (with Roy Lamson Jr) in *Harvard Studies and Notes in Philology and Literature*, XIX (1937), 199–218.

on 11 May 1668 he "went out to Mr Harris, and got him to repeat to me the words of the Echoe, while I writ them down." At least twice he went to "hear the French Eunuch sing, which we did, to our great content; though I do admire his action as much as his singing, being both beyond all I ever saw or heard" (14 October 1668). On 2 February 1668/9, attending *The Heiress*, he recorded that what "pleased me most in the play is, the first song that Knepp sings, she singing three or four; and, indeed, it is very finely sung, so as to make the whole house clap her."

The vogue of music proved a great boon to singers, lyricists, composers, and musicians. At first most of the principal singers in the theatres, such as Nell Gwyn and Mrs Knepp, were actresses doubling as vocalists, but in the last decade the demand for singers was so great that several, such as Richard Leveridge, Reading, Pate, Mrs Lindsey, and Mrs Katherine Cibber, specialized in operatic and entr'acte singing, sometimes appearing in both playhouses without having a contractual relationship with a single company. The sweeping influence of song is aptly characterized in the Epilogue to *Caligula* (1698).

> *Singing in Plays is grown so much in vogue*
> *I had some Thoughts to sing an Epilogue.*

Among the composers and musicians contributing to the taste for single songs as well as operatic works are the foremost of the age. Henry Purcell composed the music for many songs, act-tunes, overtures, and the entire music of operatic works, such as *Theodosius, The Sicilian Usurper, Sir Barnaby Whig, The English Lawyer, The Prophetess*. Many other composers assisted, perhaps less eminently but vigorously and consistently, the musical programs: John Bannister, Samuel Ackroyde, Louis Grabut, Matthew Lock, Robert Smith, Daniel Purcell, Alphonso Marsh Sr, Alphonso Marsh Jr, John Jackson, Pelham Humphrey, Roger Hill, Robert Cambert, John Blow, Robert King, Nicholas Staggins, Captain Pack, G. B. Draghi, James Hart, Thomas Farmer. Many of these, in addition to composing or performing, made a living by copying music for the orchestras. A record exists, for example, of a payment to Nicholas Staggins, Master of the King's Music, of £6 5s. and £5 12s. for preparing the music for dances, July 1675.[234] In the closing decade Daniel Purcell functioned as house composer for Drury Lane, and John Eccles held essentially the same status at Lincoln's Inn Fields.

[234] Boswell, *Restoration Court Stage*, p. 122.

CONCERTS

Concomitant with the growth of music within the theatres was the development of the public concert. The private and Court musicales continued from earlier decades, but the public concerts, particularly those which charged admission fees, was a development of the last third of the seventeenth century. John Bannister is usually credited with initiating this practice. One of his earliest public musicales was given at his home, which he called the "Musick School," situated over against the George Tavern in Whitefriars on 30 December 1672.[235] In the next winter, 1673–74, he gave several concerts, although the degree of regularity of his offerings is uncertain. Frequently throughout his career as an impresario he advertised in the *London Gazette* that he would offer a concert on a particular Thursday and every Thursday (sometimes every day) thereafter without advertising the later ones regularly. If his concerts occurred as frequently as he implied, he had during several winters a weekly concert, usually limited to an hour in the late afternoon.

He was imitated widely, both in his lifetime and later. In the season of 1677–78 Thomas Britton initiated a concert series in a loft over his warehouse in Aylesbury Street, between Clerkenwell Green and St John's Street. He had a five-stop organ, a Ruckers' virginal.[236] By 1685 this type of concert had increased in favor so markedly that these public ventures rivalled the theatres. In addition, a number of societies contributed to the vogue of vocal and instrumental musicales. There had been, ca. May 1674, a "Royal Academy of Musick," foreshadowing the highly influential Royal Academy in the first third of the eighteenth century. Very little is known of this organization, and it may have been more titular than corporate. The term appears principally in connection with a production of *Ariadne; or, The Marriage of Bacchus*, whose Dedication refers to "Your Royal Acedemy of Musick," and Louis Grabut, who composed the music, states that it was "Acted by the Royall Academy of Musick." Much more enduring was the annual Ode to St Cecilia set to music and usually performed in Stationers' Hall. The foremost poets and composers contributed to the occasion. Less important were the annual Yorkshire Feasts and the concerts of "The Lovers of Musick." Many of these concert halls and special programs imitated the theatres. Occasionally their programs included a formal Prologue and an

---

[235] For an account by a contemporary, see *Roger North on Music*, pp. 302–3.
[236] See Herbert Weinstock, *Handel* (New York, 1946), p. 54.

Epilogue. The admission charges, though often only a shilling, occasionally soared as high as a guinea, a sum higher than that which the playhouses could comfortably charge. Some of the concerts were benefits for charity, for individual singers or composers. Occasionally, as was true of the playhouses, concerts were advertised as being given for the entertainment of visiting foreigners, such as the Prince of Baden or the envoy of the Czar of Muscovy.

In the late years of the century the extravagance of the concert stage also rivalled that of the theatres, especially with respect to costs, importation of foreigners, and the addition of entertainments like the entr'acte specialties. In the closing decade several foreigners became so popular as to stimulate the satiric thrusts aimed at the vogue for foreign dancers. In the season of 1692–93, for example, an import known simply as "the Italian singer" attracted a following. Later Signor Fidelio, the singer Ramphony, and Signor Clementine, a eunuch, appeared in London to their great personal profit, some of them being advertised as having just concluded engagements on the Continent. Their salaries also became inflated. Clementine, according to the *Post Boy*, 13–15 April 1699, was to receive £500 yearly. The eunuch Francisco, according to a report mentioned by Vanbrugh, 25 December 1699, received 120 guineas for singing five times, a sum greatly contrasting with the £30 granted Thomas Dogget, returning to London, for acting five times. All of these aspects of the concert halls—the popularity of foreigners and the high financial costs particularly—were to continue into the next century.

No contemporary has left us quite so much comment upon the nature and vogue of theatrical music in the seventeenth century as Roger North. He divided his discussion between what he called "Comick" and "Opera." The former included the "common entertainement and interludes of plays, which in former times were dispersed abroad by the name of playhouse tunes. . . . There is not much to be observed of these, but onely that they are cheifly compounded of melody, and pulsation or time: the consort is not much heeded, and if the melody is ayery, or what they call pretty, the ground may be of a common style, and the more vulgar, the better."[237] North believed that some of the musicians and composers debased themselves "by turning it up to be the joy of sotts in alehouses, fair-booths, and tavernes. In a word, this sort of popular musick is most apt for driving away thinking, and letting in dancing."[238] In discussing operatic music, North referred

[237] *Roger North on Musick*, p. 271.
[238] *Ibid.*, p. 272. John Wilson, editor of this work, points out (p. 272n) that Thomas Eccles and Charles Dieupart were said to have played Corelli airs to alehouse customers and that in Tom Brown's *Dialogues from the Dead* (1702) Signor Nichola Matteis caustically censured a similar use of his own "diviner airs."

both to Restoration works and the Italian ones which became popular in the next century, and it is difficult to determine always which his comments concern. He distinguished in these the "Ayery" and the "Recitative," arguing that the recitative established a different species, so that some who are fond of the "Ayery" cannot bear "Recitative," whereas others may be wholly delighted with the latter. These distinctions "hath the same inconvenience as when (in Mr Betterton's semioperas) the drama was divided from the musick, and all the auditors were sure to be offended as well as pleased." He argued, also, that in the instrumental part "the orchestre was under based," and he discussed the comparative roles of the bassoons, the small reeds, the organ, the double viol, and the hautbois.[239]

North also concerned himself with "how and by what stepps Musick shot up in to such request, as to croud out from the stage even comedy itself, and to sit downe in her place and become of such mighty value and price as wee now know it to be."[240] In this inquiry he referred to Bannister's initiating public concerts and their influence in persuading other musicians who, having met privately to enjoy music, followed Bannister's lead for the sake of "the good half crownes [which] came in fairely."[241] As a result, North pointed out, a room in York Buildings (see the Calendar) "was built express and equipt for musick, to which was made a great resort and profit to the masters, and so might have continued but for the unfortunate interfering with the plays [an event which did not occur until the next century]. I observed well the musick here, and altho' the best masters in their turnes, as well as solo, as concerted, shewed their gifts, yet I cannot say, whatever the musick was, that the enterteinement was good; because it consisted of broken incoherent parts; now a consort, then a lutinist, then a violino solo, then flutes, then a song, and so peice after peice, the time sliding away, while the masters blundered and swore in shifting places, and one might perceive that they performed ill out of spight to one and other; whereas an enterteinment ought to proceed as a drama, firework, or indeed every publik delight, by judicious stepps, one setting off another, and the whole in a series connected and concluding in a perfect ackme, and then ceasing all at once."[242]

[239] *Ibid.*, p. 274.
[240] *Ibid.*, p. 302.
[241] *Ibid.*, p. 303.
[242] *Ibid.*, p. 305. North also described in some detail the appearance of the music room in York Buildings and the popularity of its concerts (p. 305n).

The Repertory: General View

WITH the reopening of the playhouses, the acting companies had to present old plays until new ones could be written, and the audiences were entertained with favorites of the past age, the works of Beaumont and Fletcher predominating over those by other dramatists. As Louis B. Wright has pointed out, the Restoration was particularly ready for plays by this famous pair, because during the Commonwealth the dramatic light, almost extinguished, was reinforced by a wide and deep reading of plays, of which Beaumont and Fletcher's productions proved to be favorites.[243] Printers and booksellers engaged in a brisk business with playbooks "and the reading of plays was a diversion enjoyed by many an aristocrat and liberal citizen who had no sympathy with puritan blue laws." The authorities during the Commonwealth were, in fact, so concerned with the violent antiprelatical pamphlets that they made no ordinances specifically against *belles lettres* and plays. During this period fourteen editions of *Mucidorus* appeared, eight printings of *Doctor Faustus*, six editions of *Philaster*, *A King and No King*, *The Maid's Tragedy*, and *Bussy D'Ambois*. Publishers even advertised playlists and appended them to tracts sanctioned by parliament. One lists five hundred titles. Dr. Wright notes that after 1646 dramatic publication increased, and bloomed with the publication in 1647 of the Beaumont and Fletcher *Folio*. He notes James Shirley's preface to the *Folio* as indicative of an era of playreading indoctrination: "And now Reader in this tragical age when the theatre hath been so much out-acted, congratulate thy own happiness that in this silence of the stage, thou hast a liberty to reade these immutable playes."

When the new plays appeared, they revealed the development of fairly distinctive types or sub-genres of drama. Of these, the most important were the comedy of manners, the heroic drama in rimed couplets, and musical drama. The comedy of manners, however, was not the first new form of Restoration drama. From the increased record of performances that we have compiled, the Calendar shows that it was neither the comedy of manners

---

[243] "The Reading of Plays during the Puritan Revolution," *Huntington Library Bulletin* No. 6 (1934), 72–108.

nor even the rimed heroic drama that emerged first; it was, instead, a type of comedy which may be called the Spanish romance. This kind of play, based upon a Spanish source, placed its emphasis upon a rigid code of conduct, had a plot filled with intrigue, and emphasized one or more high-spirited women in the *dramatis personae*. In this category falls Sir Samuel Tuke's *The Adventures of Five Hours*, then attributed to Calderón, which became the first highly successful drama of the Restoration. Written at the request of Charles II, Tuke's play opened on 8 January 1662/3 before a full house and achieved an excellent run of thirteen consecutive perform-ances.[244] Pepys, Evelyn, and Downes testify to the sensational impact of this work.[245] Other plays in the same category that soon followed were Lord Digby's *Elvira* (November 1664), Thomas Porter's *The Carnival* (ca. 1664), John Dryden's *The Rival Ladies* (June 1664), and, later, St Serfe's *Tarugo's Wiles* (5 October 1667) and Dryden's *An Evening's Love* (12 June 1668). The reliance upon an intrigue plot became the chief characteristic in the hands of later writers in this mode, such as Mrs Aphra Behn.

Meanwhile, the rimed heroic drama was making its way onto the stage. Roger Boyle, Earl of Orrery, is generally credited as its originator so far as composition is concerned,[246] but the approach of stage history shows that *The Indian Queen*, by John Dryden and Sir Robert Howard, was the first rimed heroic drama produced in the London theatres. Performed on 25 January 1663/4 and acted frequently through the rest of the winter, *The Indian Queen* appeared well in advance of Orrery's *The History of Henry the Fifth*, which had its première on 13 August 1664. More heroic plays by Orrery, by Dryden, and by other authors followed thick and fast. The number of these compositions, their fashionable status, as attested by con-temporary comment, and the frequency of production all emphasize the popularity of this type of drama. The Duke of Buckingham's *The Rehearsal* (7 December 1671), amusing and popular as it was, did not put an end to the rimed heroic play. Drawcansir may have slain all his opponents at one blow, but the Duke of Buckingham was not equally successful in extermin-ating the object of his ridicule. Dryden's renunciation of rime after *Aureng Zebe* (16 November 1675) led to a sharp diminution of new heroic plays, although other playwrights, especially Elkanah Settle and Nathaniel Lee, continued in this form. Even with a reduction in the number of new rimed heroic plays the records of performances show that several examples of

[244] Nicoll, *Restoration Drama*, p. 9, and Downes, *Roscius Anglicanus*, pp. 22–23.
[245] See under 8 January 1662/3 in the Calendar.
[246] For a survey of studies on this subject, see Nicoll, *Restoration Drama*, pp. 100–131.

the type remained in stock into the early eighteenth century. In fact, as one consults the records throughout the volumes of the present work he will note further examples of the continued popularity of a burlesque and the plays it mocked. Audiences, for example, flocked to applaud *The Beggar's Opera* yet continued to attend the Italian opera. *Tom Thumb* had an immediate success, but spectators still attended productions of the antique tragedies Fielding satirized. Sheridan's *The Critic* was also a stage hit, yet we see no slackening in the number of performances of Cumberland's heavy dramas.

THE COMEDY OF MANNERS

The outstanding contribution of Restoration drama to posterity was the comedy of manners.[247] It is instructive to see from the Calendar of Performances how this type of play emerged to reach its characteristic form. As noted before, the first new type of comedy has been characterized as the Spanish romance. Many of its features appear in an early comedy set not in Spain but in Italy, Richard Rhodes' *Flora's Vagaries* (3 November 1663). This rollicking play presents a strict code of parental authority and rigid social patterns, two vivacious young ladies in rebellion, plot situations in which people act artificially against normal human nature, and witty dialogue arising from the lively repartee of the heroine, Flora. In addition, and of considerable significance in the development of this genre, the women's roles were played by actresses. When Pepys saw it on 5 October 1667, Nell Gwyn and Mrs Knepp almost drove the dazzled diarist out of his mind, they excited him so.

In June 1664 Dryden's *The Rival Ladies* appeared. Made up largely of the distinguishing features cited for *Flora's Vagaries*, it introduced "the Gay Couple," a pair bound to please as Shakespeare had shown in *Love's Labors Lost* and *Much Ado About Nothing*, but bound henceforth on a new career of exploitation. On 30 July 1663 came the first full-length presentation of a fop, in James Howard's *The English Monsieur*. In March 1664 Sir George Etherege, in *The Comical Revenge*, included three pictures of contemporary

---

[247] For studies on the theory and social mode of the comedy of manners, see Nicoll, *Restoration Drama*, pp. 280–83. To his references should be added David S. Berkeley, "The Penitent Rake in Restoration Comedy, "*Modern Philology*, XLIX (1952), 223–33; T. H. Fujimura, *The Restoration Comedy of Wit* (Princeton, New Jersey, 1952); David S. Berkeley, "The Art of Whining Love," *Studies in Philology*, LII (1955), 478–96 and "Préciosité and the Restoration Comedy of Manners," *Huntington Library Quarterly*, XVIII (1955), 109–28; N. N. Holland, *The First Modern Comedies* (Cambridge, Mass., 1959).

London life with one from heroic drama. A minor writer, Thomas St Serfe, attempted something similar in *Tarugo's Wiles* (5 October 1667), where the greater part of the play is a romance set in Spain, but where one highly satiric scene is located in a London coffee house. All that remained for the complete domestication of the form was for a dramatist to drop the far-off setting and place the action in London. Impetus possibly came from France where the great dramatist Molière was producing his comic masterpieces in Paris. Apart from what Englishmen may have seen when visiting the Comédie Française, several of Molière's plays, notably *L'école des maris* and *L'école des femmes*, were quickly drawn upon by Flecknoe, Dryden, Shadwell, Sedley, and Wycherley, to be used in their own forthcoming plays.[248] In addition to what English dramatists may have learned by way of technique from Molière, they could see in his plays wit-comedy and sex-comedy placed in a contemporary setting.

All these strands came together on 6 February 1667/8 at the première of Etherege's *She Would if She Could*, for a new kind of comedy had been realized, even though the first performance was badly done and was disappointing to the spectators. A comedy of manners had arrived, which was to rise and flourish, with an *annus mirabilis* of its own in 1676, when London audiences saw the premières of Etherege's *The Man of Mode*, Shadwell's *The Virtuoso*, and Wycherley's *The Plain Dealer*. Then, just as suddenly, the era concluded. For the next fifteen years Londoners were to see many new comedies, but they were not in the genre of the comedy of manners. There were racy ones like Ravenscroft's *The London Cuckolds*, or intrigue plays by Mrs Behn, or plays in the Jonsonian tradition of the comedy of humors, and even dramas which signal the beginning of sentimental comedy. Etherege and Wycherley had ceased to write, and the younger dramatists composed other types of plays. From this hiatus, then, we can see that the comedy of manners occupied not one period but two distinct eras. The first, as we have seen, extended from 1668 through 1676; the second was not to come until 1691 and was to occupy the last decade of the century.

The second era began and ended with a stage failure. The play which started the series was Thomas Southerne's *The Wives Excuse* (December 1691). In the next season Congreve's first play, *The Old Batchelor*, appeared, to be followed in October 1693 by *The Double Dealer*, and in April 1695 by *Love for Love*, a great success. Following these came the spirited comedies of Vanbrugh, *The Relapse* and *The Provoked Wife*. Another new comic dramatist,

---

[248] See John Wilcox, *The Relation of Molière to Restoration Comedy* (New York, 1938) and Nicoll, *Restoration Drama*, pp. 186–90.

George Farquhar, began his career with *Love and a Bottle* and *The Constant Couple*, the latter having a great run. The last two plays in the tradition, Burnaby's *The Reformed Wife* and Congreve's *The Way of the World*, appeared in March 1700. The town did not receive them with praise. *The Way of the World* was not withdrawn after the first night, and the entries of its performances in the Calendar should prove a corrective to the accounts which suggest a full disaster on the first night. Congreve's masterpiece was acted again, but it was not a popular success. The second phase of the comedy of manners had ended, and the genre was to become dormant, waiting for other Irishmen to reach the London stage.

MUSICAL DRAMA

Experiments with musical drama led to the evolution of an art form that was to be unique in the history of the English theatre—dramatic opera. Not many musical dramas were produced, and of these some were termed operas which should more properly be called masques. Furthermore, it is still not clear exactly how much of the development of dramatic opera was accidental and how much was designed.[249] Four years before the return of Charles II, Sir William Davenant had contrived a species of musical drama in *The First Days Entertainment at Rutland House* and *The Siege of Rhodes* with the main purpose of offering an entertainment that would not be blocked by Puritan regulations against the stage. Following the Restoration, there was no need to take such precautions, and for some years musical drama was neglected by authors other than Davenant and Flecknoe. The next stage came with the alteration of *Macbeth* and *The Tempest* in 1673 and 1674 into elaborate, expensive spectacles which were called operatic, and with the production of Shadwell's *Psyche* and Charles Davenant's *Circe* in 1675 and 1677. All of these pieces attracted much attention and, to judge from contemporary comment, were quite popular with the audience, but as Allardyce Nicoll points out, they could not be produced very frequently because of managerial objections to the high costs of staging.[250] Dryden also turned his attention to this genre and worked with musical drama until he achieved a separate and distinct form in *King Arthur* (1691), to

[249] The most precise account of dramatic opera may be found in Eugene Haun's "The Libretti of the Restoration Opera in English," an unpubl. diss. (University of Pennsylvania, 1954). See also R. E. Moore, *Henry Purcell and the Restoration Theatre* (Cambridge, Mass., 1961) and Lincoln, "Eccles and Congreve: Music and Drama on the Restoration Stage," pp. 7–18.
[250] *Restoration Drama*, p. 158.

which he gave the name of dramatic opera. Nahum Tate's *Dido and Aeneas*, with the music composed by Henry Purcell, had appeared in a school concert two years earlier, but it was not to be performed professionally until 1700. Both pieces attracted comment, and in the last ten years of the century some five or six more dramatic operas appeared. With the death of Henry Purcell and the adoption of Italian opera, the movement ended.

In addition to discussing the new types of drama originating in this period, something should be said about the proportion of new plays to the total repertory. For a land that had been without legitimate drama for eighteen years, the number of playwrights submitting manuscripts soon after the Restoration seems fairly large. By the season of 1662–63 several important and popular new pieces had been staged, but the real increase came in the following season, when sixteen works had premières.[251] For the next few years about a dozen new plays came out each season. Then, in the season of 1676–77, the crest of the first phase of the comedy of manners, a total of twenty-three new works appeared on the stage. Few were destined to endure, but the total number is striking. Some fifteen or more new pieces were produced in each of the next four years, but a decline set in with the union of the two companies in 1682. From 1683 to 1686 only three or four new plays appeared, as the United Company held to stock and revived old plays. In the season of 1686–87, partly because of the troubled times in England, only two new plays were staged. Slowly, after the political crisis had passed and the patrons returned to the theatres, more new plays came to be offered. Eleven premières occurred in the season of 1689–90, fourteen in the following season. Still, the real spurt did not occur until Betterton defected from Drury Lane in 1695 and two companies again competed. In the season of 1695–96, the number of new plays reached a total of twenty-five, the highest figure during the Restoration. Few of these dramas had lasting merit, but competitive houses offered a dramatist at least a chance of getting a hearing for his manuscript. About twenty new plays appeared in each of the next two seasons, with an improvement in quality, as Congreve, Vanbrugh, and Farquhar were among the authors represented.

Other patterns appear when we examine the ratio of old plays to new ones. In the season of 1661–62, as might be expected, among the known

---

[251] The statistics in this paragraph and the following ones are not entirely reliable in that we still do not know the dates of the premières of some new plays and have had to place them in a specific season when they may very well have been produced a year earlier or later. Worse yet, some titles have not been identified, and these may refer to dramas better known under other titles. In addition, we cannot be certain how many old plays were revived without positive evidence for their survival being extant.

performances 54 pre-Restoration plays vied with 4 new ones. In the season of 1667–68, when we have a relatively full list of performances, the proportion was: 33 pre-Restoration dramas, 20 plays brought out since 1660, 12 new ones. Although the records are incomplete, the theatres had struck a balance among the 65 plays, so that half were new or recent. Of 54 plays known to have been staged in the season of 1674–75, the proportion was: 25 old, 16 recent productions, 13 new. Two seasons later, when many new plays appeared, 9 were old, 19 recent, and 23 new. Certainly many more old plays must have been performed of which we have no record, but new and recent dramas dominated the repertory. If we examine the records of all productions, admittedly incomplete, during the forty years from 1660 to 1700, the companies produced approximately 440 plays which can be called new or sufficiently altered to seem to be the work of a contemporary author. By contrast, approximately 120 old plays, in relatively unaltered state, completed the repertory of the Restoration period.[252]

Of the older drama, the most popular were those plays attributed to Beaumont and Fletcher. The great number of entries for these plays in the Calendar of Performances at once supports and illustrates Dryden's statements in his *Essay of Dramatic Poesy* on the vogue of the Beaumont and Fletcher plays. During the forty years from 1660 to 1700, 39 were certainly acted and 3 more may have been.[253] *The Wild Goose Chace, Philaster, Rule a Wife and Have a Wife, A King and No King,* and *The Humorous Lieutenant* were great favorites and appeared year after year. The greatest number were produced in the opening years, with 16 in the season of 1660–61 and 15 in the following season. Even after the age had acquired its own drama, eleven were in the active repertory in the season of 1668–69 and nine in that of 1686–87. Moreover, most of these were produced in unaltered form, and Arthur Colby Sprague has shown that only one-third were revised for the Restoration theatres, most of these coming late in the period.[254]

The fortunes of the plays of Shakespeare were quite different. At first sight, the cumulative total of twenty-six of his plays acted during the age seems impressive, but analysis of the statistics shows a less favorable view. The cast for a production of *The Comedy of Errors* seems to be definitely for a non-London company, and there is only a lone allusion to *Pericles*. Whereas half of the works in the Beaumont-Fletcher canon came into the repertory

252 These figures refer to the professional theatres and do not include plays which were performed solely at Court or which exist in manuscript without clear evidence of production.

253 For the full list, see the Index.

254 For details, see Professor Sprague's excellent study, *Beaumont and Fletcher on the Restoration Stage* (Cambridge, Mass., 1926).

in the opening years of the Restoration, the plays of Shakespeare appeared a few at a time, with some of these soon discarded. When we examine the year-by-year performances, we find that the highest known total in any season was only six, and this number was reached only twice. In the season of 1668–69, one of the relatively full seasons in the Calendar, six appeared. Late in the period, in the season of 1694–95, when Betterton and the leading actors formed a second company, the remaining Drury Lane actors resorted to a revival of Shakespearean drama. Six plays are on the record, but from the way Colley Cibber speaks, there may have been more.[255] Finally, the great bulk of the plays were produced in greatly altered fashion, as is well known to all students of the period.[256]

The adaptations did not set in at once. Oddly enough, the records of the season of 1660–61 show performances of four of the unrevised plays: *Hamlet*, *1 Henry IV*, *The Merry Wives*, and *Othello*. This situation did not last long, as the alterations began in the next season with Davenant's *The Law Against Lovers*. Three more relatively unaltered plays were also given during the period: *Henry VIII*, *Richard III*, and *Twelfth Night*. *Richard III* was to be revised by Colley Cibber, but not until 1700, and Shakespeare's play may have been in stock before that date.

The selection of Shakespeare's plays for the repertory and the reasons for most of the adaptations can be explained by a study of stage history. With so many new comedies written every year, there was little room or need for Shakespeare's. If one turns to the season of 1676–77, in which, as already noted, twenty-three new plays appeared (including *The Plain Dealer*, *The Rover*, and *The Fond Husband*) he will see such contemporary comedies as *The Man of Mode*, *Secret Love*, *Flora's Vagaries*, *The Cutter of Coleman Street*, *Epsom Wells*, *The Adventures of Five Hours*, and *The Sullen Lovers*. Again, in looking at the records of performances in the season of 1690–91, one will see that seven new comedies appleared, including *Amphitryon*, *The Scowrers*, and *Greenwich Park*, together with eighteen other contemporary comedies, such as *The Virtuoso*, *The Rover*, *Secret Love*, *Sir Martin Mar-All*, *An Evening's Love*, *The Kind Keeper*, and *Marriage a la Mode*.

Although more new tragedies than comedies were written during the Restoration, a majority of the tragedies were failures or at least not sufficiently popular to go into stock. Accordingly, the urgent need for different plays offered Shakespearean tragedy a place. Thus, in the early years *Hamlet*,

255 *Apology*, I, 201–2.
256 The fullest study is by Hazelton Spencer, *Shakespeare Improved* (Cambridge, Mass., 1927). See also A. H. Scouten, "The Increase in Popularity of Shakespeare's Plays in the Eighteenth Century," *Shakespeare Quarterly*, VII (1956), 189–202.

Julius Caesar, *Othello*, and *Romeo and Juliet* appear on the play lists. Toward the end of the period, as the heroic drama declined, more Shakespearean tragedies were added. When the vogue for opera emerged, plays like *Macbeth* and *The Tempest* were, as noted, natural choices for adaptation. Allardyce Nicoll has pointed out that the history plays could easily be turned into political parallels with contemporary application; an explanation, thus, is apparent for the selection and alterations of *Richard* II, *Coriolanus*, and the *Henry* VI plays.[257]

A final reason for the adaptation of Shakespeare's plays arises from the presence of actresses to play women's parts. Professional dramatists of the Restoration composed plays with the personnel of the King's Company and the Duke's Company in mind, just as Shakespeare did for his own company. It follows that Davenant, Dryden, Shadwell, Tate, and Crowne would expand the role of women in a Shakespearean text or add women's parts if they were not already there. Devotees of the Bard may object, but we are concerned here with an example of how stage history may explain a phenomenon that has puzzled some students of the period. If Otway wrote parts expressly for Mrs Barry and if Congreve designed roles for Mrs Bracegirdle to create on the stage, it is no surprise to find that other dramatists did the same in preparing a work of Shakespeare's for a new production.

Surprise may be registered, however, at the place of Ben Jonson in the repertory. From the universal chorus of adulation for the work of this Elizabethan dramatist that extends throughout the period and from the repeated references to scenes in his plays, one would certainly have expected to see his plays carried in stock. And they may have been, as fifteen titles were distributed between the King's Company and the Duke's Company. Nevertheless, our Calendar of Performances shows no increase in the known productions of Jonson's plays. Performances are recorded for only seven of his dramas (*Bartholomew Fair*, *Catiline*, *Every Man in his Humour*, *Every Man Out of his Humour*, *The Alchemist*, *The Silent Woman*, and *Volpone*) and only the last three of these appeared with any frequency. Further research, hopefully, may disclose additional productions.[258]

---

257 *Restoration Drama*, p. 173.
258 For an account of Ben Jonson, see R. G. Noyes, *Ben Jonson on the English Stage 1660–1776* (Cambridge, Mass., 1935).

John Harris's *BOOTH*,
in Bartholomew-Fair *between the* Hospital-
gate *and* Duck-lane-end, *next the* Rope-dancers,
is to be seen,

THe Court of *King Henry the Second*; And the Death
of Fair *Rosamond*: With the merry Humours of
Punchinello, and the *Lancashire*-Witches. As also the famous History of *Bungs* and Frier *Bacon*: With the merry
Conceits of their Man *Miles*. And the brazen speaking Head; wherein is represented the manner how
this Kingdom was to have been walled in with *Brass*.
Acted by Figures as large as Children two years old.

☞ *Mistake not the Booth*; *you may know it
by the* Brazen Speaking Head *in the*
Gallery.

This **ADVERTISEMENT OF A PUPPET SHOW**, now in the *Harvard Theatre Collection*,
one of the earliest playbills extant. The pieces to be shown were called drolls.

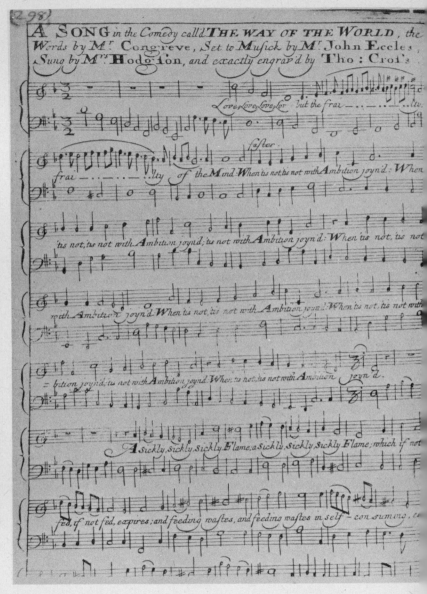

Late in the century, interest in theatre music increased, and printers began to offer popular songs from current plays in separate issue. *From the Harvard Theatre Collection.*

THOMAS BETTERTON was the greatest of the Restoration actors. *From a mezzotint by R. Williams in the Harvard Library, done after the painting by Kneller.*

Greenhill pinx   Mr Harris acting Card Woolsey

The popular actor, HENRY HARRIS, friend of Pepys and of Charles II, is shown
here in the rôle of Cardinal Wolsey in *Henry VIII*. *Courtesy of the Harvard Library.*

The Indian Queen

Smith ex.   W. Vincent sc.

MRS ANNE BRACEGIRDLE as the Indian Queen. *From a mezzotint by J. Smith in the Harvard Library.*

THE
True Lovers Tragedy:

Being an Incomparable Ballad of a Gentleman and his Lady,
That both Killed themselves for Love, under the disguised Names of

Philander and Phillis.

Phillis Philanders scattered Garments finds,
And thinks him slain, for which with Fate she joyns,
And with her Fatal Poniard striketh deep,
As Life no longer can it's station keep,
The Crimsoe Streams so fast flowd from her Veins,

Yet Dying, of her Loves dear loss complains:
No sooner Death had closed up her Starry eyes,
But her return'd Philander her espyes;
And finding that for him she lost her breath,
He kills himself, and crowns his Love with death.

To the Tune of, *Ah Cruel Bloody Fate.*

Her Ponyard then she took,
   and held it in her hand,
Then with a dying look,
   cry'd thus I Fate command:
Philander ! ah my Love I come,
   to meet the shade below ;
      Ah ! I come she cry'd,
      with a wound so wide,
   There needs no second blow.

Then Purple Wakes of Blood,
   ran streaming down the floor,
Unmov'd she saw the Flood,
   and bless'd her dying hour:
Philander, and Philander still,
   the bleeding Phillis cry'd,
      She wept a while,
      and force'd a smile,
   then clos'd her Eyes and dy'd.

AH Cruel Bloody Fate,
   what canst thou now do more?
Alas 'tis now too late,
   Philander to Restore ;
Why shou'd the Heavenly powers perswade,
   Poor Mortals to believe,
      That they guard us here,
      And reward us there,
   Yet all our joys deceive:

Upon the Blushing Ground,
   stain'd with her Virgin blood,
She lay in Deaths deep Swound,
   close by the murmering Flood :
Which for the lovely Phillis sake,
   complain'd of cruel fate,
      Which had caus'd such care,
      as had wrought despair,
   I weep it to relate.

A BLACK-LETTER BROADSIDE, presumably by Nathaniel Lee, from Act v of *Theodosius*.
In the Harvard Theatre Collection.

The veteran character actor CAVE UNDERHILL, shown in the rôle of Obadiah in Sir Robert Howard's comedy *The Committee*. The mezzotint by R. B. Parkes after the painting by R. Bing. *Courtesy of the Harvard Library.*

Anthony Leigh or the Spanish fryer

The famous comedian ANTHONY LEIGH is shown here in the
rôle of Dominic in Dryden's *The Spanish Friar*. The mezzotint
is by J. Smith, after the painting by Kneller. *Courtesy of the
Harvard Library.*

The Repertory: Specialties

HAMLET'S "The Play's the thing," now a commonplace for theatrical historians and critics, was amply exemplified in the Restoration theatre, for the center of the program was the comedy, tragedy, or dramatic opera. Nevertheless, the managers, the Court, and public entertainments throughout London provided a variety of specialties, some closely related to the drama, others possessing dramatic elements but very loosely related to the characteristics of the best dramatic fare. Some of the specialties discussed in this section are integral parts of the daily programs of the professional theatres; others made sporadic appearances there; still others competed with the offerings in the playhouses.

PROLOGUES AND EPILOGUES

Among the specialties in the professional theatres, the Prologue and the Epilogue held the most substantial place. Nearly every new play had a Prologue and an Epilogue written expressly for it; and where either is missing for a new drama, it is likely that one existed at the première but has since been lost. The audience expected these capsules of information and comment for new plays and for many old and newly revived ones. In addition, a special occasion, such as the attendance of the King or Queen, the opening of a new theatre, a performance at Court, created an excuse for the writing and speaking of fresh examples of these components of the program.[259]

The Prologue and Epilogue formed a frame in which to present the day's program. After the orchestra completed its overtures, a player stepped forth and spoke the Prologue, the curtain opening as he concluded. Ordinarily the curtain was not closed until the end of the program, the Epilogue signalling the end of the performance. Although there is no certainty that a Prologue or an Epilogue was spoken at every performance of every play, whether old

---

[259] In addition to the Prologues and Epilogues printed in editions of Restoration plays, one should examine the large and interesting collection, *Rare Prologue and Epilogues, 1642–1700*, edited by Autrey N. Wiley (London, 1940).

or new, the probability is that they were—if only to quiet the house before the curtain rose and to send it away in good humor. It may well be that, lacking an occasion for a newly written Prologue, an old one was recited at revivals, even a decade or so later. Many comments testify to the spectators' expectation of hearing these opening and closing orations. As the Prologue to *Pastor Fido* (1675) states it: "Preface and Prologue, are such modish Toys / Books ar'nt without this, nor without that Plays." That for Mrs Behn's *The Amorous Prince* frankly acknowledges that players and dramatists accede to the expectation of the spectators: "Well! you expect a Prologue to the Play, / And you expect it too Petition way." Pepys makes perfectly clear that the Prologue or Epilogue to a new play was likely to be spoken throughout the initial run. On 1 August 1668, attending *The Old Troop* for the second time, he came early to hear the Prologue, for he had arrived late and missed it on the previous performance. Downes emphasized the same point, mentioning that the Prologue to *The Woman Made a Justice* (19 February 1669/70) was spoken on each day of its fourteen consecutive performances.[260]

Even though proof is lacking that Prologue and Epilogue formed part of every performance, some commentators, seemingly bored with the practice, suggest that the repetition was tiresome. The Prologue to *The Rival Ladies* (ca. June 1664) may be a case in point.

> *'Tis much Desir'd, you Judges of the Town*
> *Would pass a vote to put all Prologues down;*
> *For who can show me, since the first were Writ,*
> *They e'r Converted one hard-hearted Wit.*

Although the tone of Dryden's Prologue is playful, that for *Tryphon*, 8 December 1668, which Pepys heard spoken at the première, is much more specific.

> *Would you decree (what I for them implore)*
> *Poets with Prologue ne're should meddle more,*
> *'Tis the best thing you for your selves could do,*
> *For Prologues first tire Poets and then you.*

Yet Pepys, for reasons he does not clearly outline, thought this "prologue most silly."

Since the intent of the Prologue was to gain the attention of the audience and the Epilogue to win applause in dismissing the auditors, the writer of each, but especially of the opening statement, must find means of making

[260] *Roscius Anglicanus*, p. 30.

an original or palatable appeal. As a result, in many Prologues the same basic approach was handled in a variety of rhetorical ways. One device was to establish a parallel to the relationship of poet / players to audience, a technique most useful for premières. For example, the Prologue to *The Life of Mother Shipton* (acted probably between 1668 and 1671) likened the theatrical situation to that of host and guests or chef and diners: "His [the poet's] is an invitation to a feast / He hopes your stomacks will not ill digest." For *The Fatal Jealousie*, 3 August 1672, the Prologue flatters the audience as possessing the status of a monarch, the author and players presenting their "low Submission," and that to *The Loyal Brother*, ca. February 1681/2, altered the comparison by referring to poets as "Lawfull Monarchs" who ruled until "Criticks, like Damn'd Whiggs, debauch'd our Age." At *The Rival Queens*, 17 March 1676/7, the Prologue suggests that bringing on a new play is like issuing a challenge to a duel or an encounter.

> *You think y'are challeng'd in each new Play-bill,*
> *And here you come for tryal of your Skill;*
> *Where, Fencer-like, you one another hurt.*

The Prologue to *The Committee*, 27 November 1662, compares a play and playwright to a tradesman selling his wares; that of *The Unhappy Favourite*, ca. October 1681, develops the parallel of the poet to the merchant, who must seek "Credit" in his "Venture." At *The Usurper*, 2 January 1663/4, the poet is likened to a pilot steering his vessel through a potentially stormy audience, whereas the Prologue to *Mithridates*, ca. February 1677/8, compares the playwright to a general marshalling his squadrons, and that for *A Commonwealth of Women*, ca. August 1685, has the speaker come forth like a champion ready to defend the author. Discussing the suitable techniques for catching the audience's frame of mind, Dryden, in the Prologue to *Secret Love* (2 March 1666/7), argued:

> *The most compendious method is to rail:*
> *Which you so like, you think your selves ill us'd*
> *When in smart Prologues you are not abus'd.*
> *A civil Prologue is approv'd by no man;*
> *You hate it as you do a Civil woman:*
> *Your Fancy's pall'd, and liberally you pay*
> *To have it quicken'd, ere you see a Play.*

Frequently an Epilogue, written, of course, before the verdict of the première was known, used a similar appeal. The Epilogue to William

Cartwright's *The Ordinary*, ca. January 1670/1, compared the play-play-wright-actors versus the spectators to sailors in a naval engagement, who, fearing the thunder and lightning and seeking shelter, desire the mercy of the elements to keep them from disaster. That for *The Widow* (in *London Drollery*, 1673) argued that "The Stage is like a Gaming-house" where the company puts up "a poor old Play" and invites the spectators to "throw out for this one stake." The Epilogue to *The Comical Revenge*, March 1664, employed another familiar comparison.

> *Like Pris'ners, conscious of th'offended Law,*
> *When Juries after th'Evidence withdraw;*
> *So waits our Author between hope and fear,*
> *Until he does your doubtful Verdict hear.*

Many an Epilogue had a wry note, no doubt, as the speaker, knowing the play had failed, uttered the hopeful, pleading words to an audience thoroughly bored and hostile. Even more embarrasing was the actor's turn to announce an additional performance of the damned play on the following day.

Because the pleading Prologue or Epilogue, regardless of the skill of the author, tended toward repetition of the obvious, playwrights often used them as a means of discussing political and literary matters or even the state of the theatre. As is well known, John Dryden frequently used the Prologue as a forum for a discussion of the playwrights of the preceding age, of the use of rhyme in drama, and of the principles of taste and criticism which he wished to establish. A Prologue spoken on a special occasion offered an opportunity to vary the tone and to flatter influential auditors, and many special ones were presented. Dryden's Prologue on the Duke of York's return from Scotland (21 April 1682) and Otway's Epilogue to a performance of *Venice Preserv'd* on that date celebrated a Tory victory and were "Recommended to All men of Sense and Loyalty" in *The Observator*, 27 April 1682. In 1682 when the two companies united, Dryden wrote a Prologue (spoken by Betterton) and an Epilogue (spoken by Smith) to welcome the King and Queen to the theatre. When a company acted in the summer at Oxford Dryden frequently wrote a Prologue or an Epilogue, sometimes comparing London and Oxford audiences or their tastes in plays. A player sometimes used one for a personal appeal, such as "Mr Haynes His Recantation-Prologue Upon his first Appearance on the Stage After His Return from Rome" (1689). Late in the century Joseph Haines and William Penkethman achieved distinction and notoriety for humorous monologues, such as "A Prologue Spoken on an Ass." One in dialogue varied the approach; Pepys enjoyed one spoken by Nell

Gwyn and Mrs Knepp on the first day of *The Duke of Lerma*, 20 February 1667/8. Another novelty appeared in the Prologue to *Calisto* (1675), performed by a Chorus and interspersed with dances.

The Epilogue followed similar patterns. If the recurrent appeal to the tender Ladies of Quality to be sympathetic grew tiresome, the playwright discussed political or literary topics or attempted a wholly new device. Henry Harris and another actor, for example, sang the Epilogue to *The Man's the Master* "like two Street Ballad-Singers,"[261] and Pepys, attending the performance, referred to "the extraordinariness of it." In fact, the Epilogue was well suited to variety, because, as the author could not certainly foresee the mood of the audience after the play, he might play it safely with novelty for an Epilogue. That for *The City Politicks* is a conversation among three actors. That for *The Island Princess* was sung by Mrs Lindsey and a "young Boy." Some took a set theme, such as William Penkethman's speaking on "The Humours of the Age." Occasionally a young child, usually a girl, warmed the hearts of the audience with youthful charm, and if the management and players wished to make the Epilogue an undeniable success, they chose Beck Marshall, Nell Gwyn, Anne Bracegirdle, or Elizabeth Barry to wheedle the spectators into a round of applause.

That the spectators gave genuine, even critical, attention to the Prologue and Epilogue has already been suggested. Pepys' response to the Prologue to *The Duke of Lerma*, 20 February 1667/8, was highly appreciative of the manner if not the content: "And Knepp and Nell spoke the prologue most excellently, especially Knepp, who spoke beyond any creature I ever heard." On the other hand, he judged the Prologue to *The Man's the Master*, 26 March 1668, to be "but poor" and found "little" in the Epilogue to enjoy except the novelty of its being sung in the mode of "Street Ballad Singers." The popularity of Prologues an Epilogues, even beyond the stage, is evident in the extremely large number of those separately printed during the late seventeenth and early eighteenth centuries. Miss Wiley's large collection testifies to a demand for broadside versions which were usually issued within a week after their presentation on stage, as indicated by Narcissus Luttrell's manuscript notations of his date of purchase. Miss Wiley's list includes about 75 separately printed Prologues and Epilogues, most of them belonging to the period from 1660 to 1700. This practice continued into the next century, but at a reduced rate of publication.

Another evidence of the popularity of these appendages to the play appears in the imitation of the theatres by the concert halls, where neither

[261] *Ibid.*

the Prologue nor the Epilogue served the same need as in the playhouse. At York Buildings, on 20 March 1699/1700 at a benefit for Mrs Hudson and Williams, Joseph Haines spoke a Prologue; on 21 June 1700 at a concert for the representatives of the Emperor of Morocco, both Prologue and Epilogue were spoken. When Dorset Garden Theatre turned to lotteries in the last decade of the seventeenth century, a Prologue to open the day's events was considered a useful, perhaps necessary, device.

The Prologue and Epilogue had other purposes and values besides initiating the program[262] and concluding with a request for applause. Writing them provided an income to the author, although the returns were not large. When Southerne at first paid Dryden to write a Prologue or an Epilogue, the charge for both was four guineas. Around 1682, however, Dryden raised his fee and charged Southerne six guineas.[263] When Cibber wrote a Prologue for the opening of Drury Lane in the spring of 1695, he "insisted that two Guineas should be the Price" of allowing it to be spoken, and he got his price. That the sum may not have been excessive is wryly suggested in the Prologue to a play acted privately, which appeared in Thomas Duffet's *New Poems* (1675).

> *Prologues, those pleasing and successful ways,*
> *To gain protection for ill written Plays.*

BALLET

The vogue of the dance, both as entr'acte entertainment or integral parts of a play, has already been discussed, but the occasional productions of specialties called "ballets" or "masques" warrants a separate entry. The ballet as an art form had not by this time become individualized or conventionalized,[264] some being referred to primarily by title without clarification or details. An example is the *Ballet de la Paix* performed in London in 1660 without indication of the circumstances or content. On 16 March 1662/3 Jacques Thierry and Will Schellinks, two foreigners visiting in London, attended what they called a "ballet" but recorded no particulars.[265] Possibly similar was a "Grand

[262] On one occasion, the première of *The Indian Queen*, 27 January 1663/4, the Prologue appears to have been spoken after the curtain was opened.

[263] Wiley, *Rare Prologues and Epilogues*, pp. 67–69.

[264] One should note also some confusion in terminology, such as Pepys' use of the phrase "in the form of a ballet" in referring to the Epilogue sung by two actors for *The Man's the Master*, 26 March 1668. Downes, *Roscius Anglicanus*, p. 30, refers to the same Epilogue as "Singing the Epilogue like two Street Ballad-Singers."

[265] Seaton, *Literary Relationships*, pp. 334, 336.

Masque" danced before Caesar and Cleopatra in *Pompey the Great*, ca. January 1663/4, but no description survives of this work by John Ogilby. Possibly more elaborate was a ballet-masque given at Court on 20 February 1670/1, which *The Bulstrode Papers* characterized as "the grand ballet," suggesting that it was an artistic unit, not simply a ball in which all participated (see the Calendar). When this work was in preparation, Girolamo Alberti, 6 February 1670/1, emphasized to his own Court that "a grand ballet" was shortly to be staged,[266] and Lady Mary Bertie, on 23 February 1670/1, stressed the richess of the costumes, the clothes being "shifted" three times, the fineness of the dancing as well as "fine musickes," including new songs.[267] Still later, possibly in February 1673/4, a *Ballet et Musique pour le divertissement du Roy de Grande Bretagne* was performed in London. An example of a masque within a play is in Act II of *Timon of Athens*, ca. January 1677/8, Downes[268] referring to "the Musick in't well Perform'd." The characters included Aegipanes, Bacchus, Cupid, shepherds, nymphs, and maenads.

The most specific statement concerning a dramatic performance of this kind was made by Cosmo the Third, attending an offering of *Love's Mistress* at the King's Theatre on 24 May 1669.

A well-arranged ballet, regulated by the sound of various instruments, with new and fanciful dances after the English manner, in which different actions were counterfeited, the performers passing gracefully from one to another, so as to render intelligible, by their movements, the acts they were representing.[269]

Occasional other references suggest artistry of a similar form, such as a portion of *The Empress of Morocco*, 3 July 1673, which Roger North characterizes as being "a sort of masque poem of Orfeus and Euridice, set by Mr M. Lock, but scandalously performed. It begins 'The Groans of Ghosts.'"[270] Although the late seventeenth century did not develop this art form meticulously, the theatres in the next century dealt with it fully and seriously.

PUPPETRY AND MECHANICAL SHOWS

These mechanic arts were primarily practiced outside the professional theatres, though not wholly so. The puppet show, popular at the Fairs, at

---

[266] *Calendar of State Papers Venetian*, 1671–72, p. 15.
[267] HMC, Rutland MSS (London, 1889), II, 222.
[268] *Roscius Anglicanus*, p. 37.
[269] *Travels of Cosmo the Third*, p. 347.
[270] *Roger North on Music*, p. 306.

Court, and in booths in Charing Cross, had its own specialist, Anthony Devoto (in many variant spellings).271 Pepys and Evelyn, as well as many others, delighted in these exhibitions in London, and on 23 September 1673 Evelyn described an extensive mechanical show in a room in Hatton Garden: "representations of all sorts of animals, handsomely painted on boards of cloth, & so cut out & made to stand & move, fly, crawl, roare & make their several cries."

Within the professional theatres puppetry was apparently limited to an occasional scene within a play. Shortly after the Restoration the best example is the puppet show in Ben Jonson's *Bartholomew Fair*. Pepys, seeing it on 7 September 1661, felt that the introduction of puppetry lessened the impact of the drama: "but I do never a whit like it the better for the puppets, but rather the worse." When he saw it a few days later, 12 September 1661, he repeated and underscored his dislike: "yet I do not like the puppets at all." There seem to have been no other puppet shows (by nonhuman figures) introduced into the dramas proper, but the influence of this type of show, as well as the puppet, Punchanello, and marionettes was, as George Speaight has amply shown, widespread through the period from 1660 to 1700.

PROCESSIONS

This type of dramatic presentation, a favorite in the eighteenth century, was not often practiced in the Restoration theatre, although occasional attempts at pageantry of this sort appear. Certainly the Lord Mayor's Day celebrations, with the long parades and the pageants devised and executed at considerable cost, gave the populace a taste for the processional. In the theatres the best example occurs in *Henry* VIII, which Pepys saw on 1 January 1663/4. Not particularly enjoying it, he considered it a series of tableaux without artistic unity: "so simple a thing made up of a great many patches, that, besides the shows and processions in it, there is nothing in the world good or well done." Count Cominges emphasized the same loosely organized episodes when he stated: "I have seen performed the whole life of Henry the Eighth,"272 and Katherine Phillips, writing on 23 January 1663/4 (see the Calendar) considered it "little better then Puppett-plays."

271 For some of the puppet shows, see the Daily Calendar, and for a full study of the puppet theatre in the late seventeenth century, see George Speaight, *The History of the English Puppet Theatre* (London, 1955), pp. 73–91.

272 Jusserand, "A French View of England in 1666," p. 794.

THE AFTERPIECE

Like the Procession, the Afterpiece, as a formal part of the repertory, held a minor place in the last forty years of the seventeenth century. Because the play, with the intervals and entr'acte entertainments, occupied about three hours and because few short works were available, the professional theatres failed to see any advantage in a double bill and the spectators did not demand one. The principal occasion on which an afterpiece appeared was a performance of two new works by Thomas Otway at the Duke's Theatre, probably in December 1676. The first play, *Titus and Berenice*, had only three short acts, and because of its brevity Otway apparently felt that a second work was needed to complete the evening. For this he wrote *The Cheats of Scapin*, a farce, which ultimately became far more popular than its twin play, a tragedy. By the end of the century the growing attention to the concept of a variety of entertainments prepared the way for the double bill, but the Afterpiece did not gain full acceptance until the early years of the eighteenth century.

DROLLS AND INTERLUDES

These entertainments principally appeared at the Fairs (see the section on the Fairs and the Daily Calendar), but on at least one occasion, 11 November 1672, Charles II through the Lord Chamberlain issued a directive allowing Antonio di Voto to "Exercise & Play all Drolls and Interludes" except that he should not encroach upon those pieces usually acted at the professional theatres.[273] Except for drolls at the Fairs, little is known of this form of entertainment.

DOUBLE VERSIONS OF A PLAY

The period of the Restoration saw a great many plays revised, even drastically altered, such as *King Lear*. Nearly all of these adaptations, as might be expected since they were altered to meet the taste of a new and different audience, drove the original version from the stage, yet on at least one occasion the theatres provided a double presentation, offering on one day

[273] Nicoll, *Restoration Drama*, p. 250.

the original play, on the following day the adaptation. It is surprising and unfortunate that neither the date of this experiment nor the text of the adaptation is known. The play was *Romeo and Juliet*, and John Downes, the prompter of the Duke's Company, is our only source of information. He reported that James Howard altered the tragedy into a tragi-comedy by "preserving Romeo and Juliet alive."[274] This type of alteration was not unusual, but the playing of these two versions may represent an experiment unique in that period: "so that when the Tragedy was Reviv'd again, 'twas Play'd Alternately, Tragical one Day, and Tragicomical another; for several Days together." As many spectators attended the theatre on several days of the week (Pepys occasionally attended three or four days in a row), one can regret that, if adaptations were the order of the day, the managers did not more often allow their audience the esthetic and critical experience of having the old and new versions placed before them in this fashion.

FOREIGN SPECIALTIES

Of considerable importance to the professional theatres, particularly as a threat to their prosperity, were the frequent appearances of foreign performers. As has already been indicated in connection with songs and dances, the individual foreigner was a popular figure, especially in the late years of the century. On the other hand, during the years immediately after the return to the throne of Charles II, the fondness of the monarch for French and Italian players prompted him to invite entire troupes to his kingdom.[275]

As early as 30 August 1661 Pepys attended a French comedy which he thought ill done, the scenes and company being "nasty and out of order and poor." Early that winter, 2 December 1661, Jean Channouveau received £300 from the King as a bounty to the French comedians.[276] Thereafter, except for occasional gaps, such as that caused by the Great Plague, foreign companies appeared regularly in England, and Charles II negotiated for others who did not accept an invitation. Troupes appeared in London in these seasons: 1660–61, 1661–62, 1663–64, 1669–70, 1671–72, 1672–73,

274 *Roscius Anglicanus*, p. 22.

275 The vogue of the foreign company during the late seventeenth century has been discussed by several scholars. For the principal studies, see Lawrence, "Early French Players in England," pp. 125–40; I. K. Fletcher, "Italian Comedians in England in the Seventeenth Century," *Theatre Notebook*, VIII (1954), 88–89; and Sybil Rosenfeld, *Foreign Theatrical Companies in Great Britain in the 17th and 18th Centuries*, The Society for Theatre Research, Pamphlet Series, No. 4 (London, 1955).

276 *Calendar State Papers, Treasury Books*, 1660–67, p. 311.

1673–74, 1674–75, 1675–76, 1676–77, 1677–78, 1678–79, 1682–83, and 1683–84. Some of these companies presented plays at Court, although we usually do not know the titles of the dramas offered; ordinarily they brought their own scenes, costumes, and decorations, as the rcords disclose orders permitting the import or export of their goods. Nearly all appeared under the express protection of the Crown, for the Lord Chamberlain or the King issued orders forbidding any one to interfere with their liberty to act. Other troupes came under the sponsorship of other persons of rank, such as the Duke of Modena's Company in 1678–79 and the Prince of Orange's troupe in 1683–84. A few individuals were men of considerable fame, such as Tiberio Fiorelli, commonly referred to as Scaramuccio, whose presence Charles II personally sought on several occasions.

These invasions of foreign troupes often affected the London companies adversely. During the height of the foreign successes Prologues and Epilogues bitterly complain of the apparent preference of the Court for non-English performers, especially when, during one visit by Fiorelli, the theatre in the Court charged admission, an act which many considered not only beneath the dignity of the Crown but a genuine injustice to the professional English companies. As the King's and Duke's companies were relatively helpless in the face of Charles II's liking for these attractions, their principal means of coping with this competition, other than ridicule and complaint, was to offer more spectacle and more entr'acte entertainments of their own. After the death of Charles II the visits of foreign companies slackened until the second decade of the eighteenth century when other monarchs, the Hanoverians this time, showed a preference for non-English performers.

The Production of Plays

THE ULTIMATE purpose, of course, of all the elements in the theatrical world—the construction of a theatre, the securing of plays, the engaging of a company, the composition of songs and dances, and the myriad details—was the production of a three-hour program, at the center of which was a carefully composed and rehearsed drama. During the Restoration, as at all times in theatrical history, this was a complex process. Unfortunately, not very much can be said about the theories of the management concerning a seasonal or long-range purpose which is not already implicit in the discussion of the repertory, the specialties, and management and operations or which will not be revealed by a careful study of the Calendar. Actually, deliberate and intensive discussion of the theory of theatrical offerings is rare at this time; and when it occurs it often, as was true with Thomas Killigrew's talks with Pepys on 12 February 1666/7, concerns the speculative future rather than an appraisal of current practices. Nevertheless, one may take Dryden's statement in the Prologue To the King and Queen, at the Opening of Their Theatre, 1682, as a mature reflection, tinged with satire, upon the role of the stage.

> Old Men shall have good old Plays to delight 'em:
> And you, fair Ladys and Gallants that slight 'em,
> We'll treat with good new Plays; if our new Wits can write 'em.
> We'll take no blundring Verse, no fustian Tumour,
> No dribling Love, from this or that Presumer:
> No dull fat Fool shamm'd on the Stage for humour.
> For, faith, some of 'em such vile stuff have made,
> As none but Fools or Fairies ever Play'd;
> But 'twas, as Shopmen say, to force a Trade.
> We've giv'n you Tragedies, all Sense defying:
> And singing men, in wofull Metre dying;
> This 'tis when heavy Lubbers will be flying.
> All these disasters we well hope to weather;
> We bring you none of our old Lumber hether:

Several of these complexities fall under the headings of securing a play, the preparing and rehearsing of the drama, the première, and the run.

SECURING A PLAY

Immediately after the Restoration, securing plays for presentation was a relatively simple task. With little incentive for writing plays during the Commonwealth, the theatres in 1660 naturally turned to the large stock handed down from Elizabethan and Jacobean times. For some years following 1660 the Lord Chamberlain regulated the division of plays among the principal companies—see, for example, the lists under 12 January 1668/9—the allotment sometimes being for a limited period. An early document dividing the stock assigned to Sir William Davenant for the Duke's Company eleven plays, principally Shakespearean.[277] These allocations may well have been made at the desire of management to secure an amicable division of the stock. That more extensive lists existed, probably from 1660, is suggested by the Lord Chamberlain's two directives in the seasons of 1667–68 and 1668–69. On 20 August 1668 his office allotted 23 plays, representing a variety of pre-Restoration authors, to the Duke's Company;[278] the order, dated 12 January 1668/9,[279] gave to the King's Company 108 plays, representing nearly all of Jonson's works and many of Shakespeare's. Although these allocations were not rigidly followed, the companies observed them with care, for the plays of Jonson, for example, appear to have been acted primarily by the King's Company before the merger of the companies in 1682.[280]

After the initial reliance upon old plays had created a repertory, the Duke's Company assumed a slight advantage in the search for new ones as Sir William Davenant, the proprietor, had several of his own available and shortly was to revise and revive some older dramas, such as *Hamlet* and *Macbeth*. Within ten years several plays became available from gentlemen and Persons of Quality who wrote for prestige without primary, if any, thought of financial gain, such as William Cavendish, Duke of Newcastle; Roger Boyle, Earl of Orrery; and John Wilmot, Earl of Rochester. Perhaps Sir George Etherege should be included among this group. Some of their plays were eminently successful; others received only passing recognition. Within a short time after the resumption of acting the professional dramatist, the most productive source of new plays, became a highly influential element

---

[277] Nicoll, *Restoration Drama*, pp. 352–53. The list also gave Davenant two months' rights to six other plays.
[278] *Ibid.*, p. 353.
[279] *Ibid.*
[280] Noyes, *Ben Jonson on the English Stage*, pp. 319–20.

in the offerings of each company. John Dryden is an illustrious example. Early in 1663 the Theatre Royal produced his first play, *The Wild Gallant*, and for many years he attached himself closely to the King's Company. At first his relationship was primarily that of a professional happily developing an association with a single company, although not exclusively contracting with it for every one of his dramas. Later this relationship became a more binding one; probably in the spring of 1668 he entered into a formal agreement to provide the company with three plays annually, the King's Company to give him one and one-quarter shares of the theatre's profits.[281] In force until 1678, this agreement created in principle the playwright-sharer, upon whose pen the theatre relied for a steady flow of new manuscripts. Dryden was unable, however, to maintain the heavy production schedule, and the complaint of several actor-sharers that Dryden had failed to keep the agreement probably reflects not only Dryden's inability but also the declining fortunes of the King's Company, a condition which made the agreement less valuable to Dryden.[282]

Nor was this arrangement between Dryden and the King's Company unique. Apparently Nathaniel Lee had a similar working agreement with the King's Company, as implied in the complaint against Dryden. At the same time John Crowne had a "like agremt" with the Duke's Company.[283] In all probability Thomas D'Urfey had a similar contract with the King's Company during part of his career, for his name appears on the company list on 8 May 1676.[284] Earlier (around 1673), according to *Reflections Upon a Late Pamphlet Intituled A Narrative Written by E. Settle* (1683), Settle had been offered by the Duke's House a yearly grant of £50 if that company "might have the Acting of all the Plays he made," but, having greater expectations from the King's Company, he allied himself with it (p. 2). At the end of the century Congreve was essentially playwright-in-residence with the company in Lincoln's Inn Fields. Whether or not formal arrangements existed, Mrs Aphra Behn, Thomas Otway, and Edward Ravenscroft had most of their plays acted by the Duke's Company.

Another arrangement was that of the actor-playwright whose works appeared under the direction of the company to which he was attached. Thomas Betterton, long a member of the Duke's Company, saw most of his plays appear in its playhouses; John Lacy, attached to the King's Company,

281 James M. Osborn, *John Dryden: Some Biographical Facts and Problems* (New York, 1940), p. 186.

282 *Ibid.*, pp. 188–89.

283 *Ibid.*, p. 188.

284 Wilson, "Players' Lists in the Lord Chamberlain's *Registers*," p. 27.

had his works produced by that company. Thomas Otway, trying out as an actor but failing, might well have become an actor-playwright had not his initial appearance on stage proved his undoing. Colley Cibber, on the other hand, began as an apprentice actor and, once secure in the profession, wrote many plays which, with rare exceptions, were produced by the Rich-Skipwith regime to which he was contracted. William Mountfort and George Powell followed similar patterns.

The majority of new plays, then, came from the expected sources: men and women closely associated with the theatres, either as independent professional dramatists, as writers under contract, or as actor-playwrights. The gentleman-dramatist had his greatest opportunities shortly after the Restoration; the professional writer early found and consistently kept his position; and in the last twenty years of the century opportunities for the actor-dramatist increased steadily. In fact, the author of *A Comparison Between the Two Stages* (1702) became quite caustic concerning the large number of actors whose plays appeared, often without success, and apparently delighted in judging as "Damn'd, Damn'd" each new failure by an actordramatist. To judge by Farquhar's remarks in *A Discourse Upon Comedy*[285] the town taunted amateur dramatists who aspired to easy fame.

'Tis then whisper'd among his Friends at Will's and Hippolito's, that Mr Such-a-one has writ a very pretty Comedy; and some of 'em, to encourage the young Author, equip him presently with Prologue and Epilogue. Then the Play is sent to Mr Rich, or Mr Betterton, in a fair legible Hand, with the Recommendation of some Gentleman, that passes for a Man of Parts, and a Critick. In short, the Gentleman's Interest has the Play acted, and the Gentleman's Interest makes a Present to pretty Miss —— she's made his Whore, and the Stage his Cully, that for the Loss of a Month in Rehearsing, and a Hundred Pound in dressing a confounded Play, must give the Liberty of the House to him and his Friends for ever after.

In addition to the contractual relationships between playwright and company, a good deal of informality took place behind the scenes in arranging for plays. Charles II, genuinely interested in the stage, sometimes assisted a playwright not only by personal and financial encouragement but also by making suggestions for plots and incidents which, the author later happily proclaimed, led to a successful première. The King ordered Sir Samuel Tuke to write *The Adventures of Five Hours*, which became a popular success, and in the Prologue spoken at Court the author stated:

[285] *Works*, I, 101.

> *Just at that time he [the author] thought to disappear;*
> *He chanc'd to hear his Majesty once say*
> *He lik'd this Plot: he staid, and writ the Play.*

Similarly John Crowne wrote *Sir Courtly Nice* at the King's suggestion but was disappointed in the King's death before the play reached the stage. Dryden, writing in July 1677 and probably referring to *Mr Limberham*, stated that "it will be almost such another piece of business as the fond Husband, for such the King will have it, who is parcell poet with me in the plott."[286]

Within and without the theatres other forces assisted in securing plays. Edward Ravenscroft, in the Epistle to the Reader in *The Careless Lovers*, 12 March 1672/3, stated that the play was "written at the Desire of the Young Men of the Stage" (Duke's Company) so that they might have a new play for their personal profit; to accommodate, them, he wrote it within a week. Many years later, after the success of Vanbrugh's *The Relapse* at Drury Lane, Lord Halifax, whose interests lay with Betterton's company at Lincoln's Inn Fields, "having formerly, by way of Family-Amusement, heard the *Provok'd Wife* read to him in its looser Sheets, engag'd Sir John Vanbrugh to revise it and gave it to the Theatre in Lincoln's-Inn Fields." On this occasion a friend of one theatre secured a potential success away from the opposition.[287]

Legal cases throw light upon other ways by which plays came to the stage. As a result of litigation we know that in October 1681 Elkanah Settle agreed with Elizabeth Leigh, a spinster, to write an interlude or drama on a subject provided by her, she to receive £20 whenever the play appeared at the Theatre Royal. Unfortunately for both, the King's Company, in financial difficulties, merged with the Duke's Company before the play could be acted. As a result, Elizabeth Leigh sued for forfeiture of the bond Settle had made. Eventually the play, under the title of *The Ambitious Slave*, was acted in 1694 and damned.[288] At one time during the late seventeenth century, however, the situation was reversed. The theatres no longer sought new plays; in fact, during the early years of the United Company management was so intent upon cutting costs and keeping the status quo that its interest in new plays flagged. The number of new plays produced dropped to two or three each season, and the action stifled the creative impulses of the playwrights and dried up the sources of new works.

[286] *The Letters of John Dryden*, pp. 11–12.
[287] Cibber, *Apology*, I, 217.
[288] Hotson, *Commonwealth and Restoration Stage*, pp. 274–76.

SECURING A PERMIT

As has already been pointed out (see the section on Management and Operations), once a play had been secured, the managers were expected, at least
in principle, to obtain a license to present it. Although many of these points
have been made in the earlier discussion of censorship, the matter needs a
brief review at this point. In 1660 Sir Henry Herbert, Master of the Revels,
fought hard to make mandatory a review of every new and revived play
by his office, for which he would receive a fee; but the principal companies
neither fully nor promptly acquiesced. The evidence indicates, nevertheless,
that some plays received Herbert's careful inspection. An example is
John Wilson's *The Cheats*, approved on 6 March 1662/3.[289] Herbert's notation
on the manuscript states: "This Comedy of the Cheates, may be Acted,
As Allowed for the Stage, the Reformations strictly observed."[290] Throughout
the play Herbert ordered deletions of words or phrases (including "Faith"
and "Abrams bosome") as well as longer passages. Although this supervision
was irritating in principle and in detail, the King's Company lacked a firm
technical basis for refusing Herbert, as Killigrew on 5 June 1662 had agreed
with the Master of the Revels for review (including a fee) of all new and
revived plays.[291]

Herbert's extensive alterations in this play make certain the existence
of the censor and the necessity for obtaining a clearance before acting;
Herbert undoubtedly exercised his powers as fully as he could until he
relinquished his office, for he was a man of set principles and dogged perse-
verance. No other examples for the first decade following the Restoration
are so detailed and clear, and the degree of surveillance of plays is in doubt.
The fact that many plays published and acted during the reign of Charles II
contain expressions which Herbert presumably would have excised suggests
that after Thomas Killigrew had succeeded Herbert as Master of the Revels,
the securing of a permit may have been a perfunctory requirement.

By the time of the Popish Plot the emphasis had changed to political
censorship, yet the fact that a number of plays appeared on the stage for
two or three performances before being banned suggests that either the
pre-production licensing was of minor importance or that the implications
of these plays did not come to full understanding until they had been acted.

[289] For a full discussion of the circumstances of this play, see an edition by M. C. Nahm
(Oxford, 1935), particularly Chapter VI.

[290] *Ibid.*, p. 124.

[291] Herbert, *Dramatic Records*, Item XXIII.

Lucius Junius Brutus and Tate's *Richard II* were acted, then prohibited, whereas Banks's *The Innocent Usurper* was, according to the author, banned by the censor some ten years before publication in 1694. His *Cyrus the Great* was apparently banished before 1681 and not acted until the season of 1695–96.

At the end of the century the systematic licensing of plays had apparently become lax, although the Master of the Revels had attempted to collect fees, for the Lord Chamberlain on 24 January 1695/6 issued an order whose preamble stated: "Whereas several playes &c are Acted & prologues spoken wherein many things ought to be struck out and corrected, And yᵉ plays approved and Licensed by yᵉ Master of the Revells according to yᵉ Antient Custome of His place and upon the Examination of the said Master."²⁹² It seems probable that the licensing and censoring of plays continued through the reign of Charles II, but the restraints probably were (except in times of political tension) lightly imposed. The situation seems to have altered after the accession of William and Mary in 1688, for the Crown showed more determination in enforcing orders against debauchery and profanity. Jeremy Collier and the Societies for the Reformation of Manners accentuated this tendency. In the midst of attacks upon the immorality of the stage and of prosecutions of players for speaking licentious lines, Nahum Tate issued, on 6 February 1699 [1699/1700 (?)], *A Proposal for Regulating the Stage & Stage-Players*. In it he suggested that supervisors of plays be appointed by the government and "that all Plays (capable of being reform'd) be rectify'd by their Authors if Living—and proper Persons appointed to Alter and reform Those of Deceased Authors and neither old or modern Plays permitted to be acted till reform'd to the satisfaction of the Sᵈ supervisors."²⁹³ At this time the censor seems to have become more strict and the licensing more consistently required. On 18 February 1698/9 the Lord Chamberlain issued a sharp order noting that "severall new & revived" plays had been acted "without any Licence" and specifying that "for yᵉ future noe playes shall be Acted but such as shall first be sent (and that in due time) to Charles Killigrew Esqʳ Master of yᵉ Revells by him to be perused and diligently Corrected & Licensed."²⁹⁴

A few examples suggest further compliance with the requirement of securing a permit. When Elkanah Settle's *The World in the Moon* was advertised in the *Post Boy*, 29 June–1 July 1697, the notice emphasized: "It is licensed

²⁹² Krutch, *Comedy and Conscience after the Restoration*, p. 180.
²⁹³ *Ibid.*, p. 177.
²⁹⁴ Nicoll, *Restoration Drama*, p. 341.

by the Lord Chamberlain's Secretary, and the Master of the Revels." On 4 March 1698/9 Dryden wrote that Congreve's *The Double Dealer* had been revived "with Several Expressions omitted,"[295] and although these changes may have been made voluntarily by the theatre, possibly they resulted from formal re-examination of the text. In discussing his difficulties with a revision of Shakespeare's *Richard III*, acted possibly in February 1699/1700, Cibber explicitly stated that "the Master of the Revels, who then licens'd all Plays for the Stage . . . would strike out whole Scenes of a vicious or immoral Character." The licenser removed the entire first act of Cibber's alteration.[296] Finally, the author of *A Comparison Between the Two Stages* (1702), in discussing the situation within the theatres, referred to the fact that "The Play was ordered to be Licenced . . . and forty [shillings] more for the Licence" (p. 8).

The fact that the files of the Master of the Revels and the Lord Chamberlain have not survived make impossible a conclusive statement concerning the theory and practice of licensing; nevertheless the theoretical and actual status seems to fall within these limits: By tradition, the Master of the Revels had the right to demand the submission of new and revived dramatic works and to charge a fee for their perusal and licensing. During the reign of Charles II the rigors of censorship were, except in times of political tension, probably technical rather than actual. After 1688 the Crown gave new strength to the censor, and according to the letter of the law, all plays, old and new, were subject to the Master of the Revels.

READING A PLAY

Once a manuscript was completed, or nearly so, it might pass through a series of readings. Of the earliest of these—that by an outsider, who, perusing the author's text, thought fit to recommend it to a company—not much is known. Nevertheless, one example has already been mentioned, Cibber's account of Lord Halifax's having read "in its looser Sheets" Vanbrugh's *The Provok'd Wife* and his recommending it to Betterton's company in the last decade of the century.[297] A much better documented case is Congreve's *The Old Batchelor*, the author's first play. When Congreve submitted it to the United Company in the season of 1692–93, it was recognized as an exceptional work possessing, nevertheless, technical deficiencies. Thomas

295 *The Letters of John Dryden*, p. 113.
296 *Apology*, I, 275.
297 *Ibid.*, I, 217.

Southerne, attracted by its unusual quality, assisted in a revision of the manuscript and left a memorandum concerning the rewriting.[298] First, the comedy was brought to the attention of Dryden, "who upon reading it sayd he never saw such a first play in his life." Then Dryden, Arthur Mainwaring, and Southerne "red it with great care," Dryden putting the scenes in the order in which they were acted.

Both Southerne and Dryden participated in the initial stages of securing and reading manuscripts on other occasions. When Cibber had *Love's Last Shift* in a final draft, he had difficulty in getting it accepted; he turned to Southerne, who "having had the Patience to hear me read it to him, happened to like it so well that he immediately recommended it to the Patentees."[299] On 11 April 1700, Dryden, writing about Southerne's *The Fate of Capua*, implied that he had frequently assisted authors by reading their manuscripts and securing them a hearing. On this occasion, however, he pointed out that he was "out with that Company, & therefore if [he] can help it, will not read it before tis Acted; though the Author much desires [he] shou'd."[300]

Members of the companies also performed a similar service. Numerous authors paid tributes in the prefaces to their published plays to the kindness and skill with which Betterton, usually in his capacity as a manager, had read and improved their plays. Perhaps most of this attention occurred during the rehearsal and staging, but Betterton probably was often approached to read and "correct" a play. Similarly, William Mountfort apparently took over an almost completed manuscript occasionally and adapted it for production, with the result that sometimes, as with the play of *Henry II*, it is difficult to know who actually wrote it. The author of *A Comparison Between the Two Stages* (1702) seized upon this practice as the basis for a satiric thrust at playwrights and managers. Alleging that his example actually happened, one of the commentators in this work reported (p. 8):

The thing is this; A Gentleman carry'd a Play there [Drury Lane], a Day was appointed for the reading; a Dinner was bespoke at a Tavern for half a Score, at least that number came to judge his Play, tho' not three of 'em cou'd tell the difference between Comedy and Tragedy; in the reading of it (that is after Dinner) most of 'em dropt off, but two remain'd to hear it out, and then they walkt; so that there was but the Gentleman and his Friend left, and not a Penny all this while paid towards the Reckoning. The Play was ordered to be Licenced, so that forty Shillings

298 Hugh Macdonald, *John Dryden: A Bibliography of Early Editions and of Drydeniana* (Oxford, 1939), p. 54n.
299 *Apology*, I, 212.
300 *The Letters of John Dryden*, p. 136.

for the Dinner, and forty more for the Licence, made just four Pounds, so much it cost him already.

Once a play was ready for casting and production, the play was commonly read aloud to the assembled actors. Sometimes the author read his own work. Cibber testified to Nathaniel Lee's ability:

On the contrary, Lee, far [Dryden's] inferior in Poetry, was so pathetick a Reader of his own Scenes, that I have been inform'd by an Actor who was present, that while Lee was reading to Major Mohun at a Rehearsal, Mohun, in the Warmth of his admiration, threw down his Part and said, Unless I were able to play it as well as you read it, to what purpose should I undertake it?[301]

Cibber also testified to Dryden's following the same practice, though not so skillfully. Writing about the rehearsal of *Amphitryon*, produced on 21 October 1690, Cibber stated:

When he brought his Play of *Amphytrion* to the Stage, I heard him give it his first Reading to the Actors, in which, though it is true he deliver'd the plain Sense of every Period, yet the whole was in so cold, so flat, and unaffecting a manner, that I am afraid not being believ'd when I affirm it.[302]

CASTING AND REHEARSAL

Relatively little evidence has survived concerning the formal procedures in casting plays, new or old, following the Restoration. At first, with a limited number of actors, casting was based, of course, upon the older and experienced men like Charles Hart and Michael Mohun, who had played before 1660. In addition, until actresses appeared on the London stage, the women's roles were assigned to the "boy actors," such as William Betterton, Edward Kynaston, James Nokes, or Edward Angel. Once the two principal companies had been systematically organized, with actresses added to their rosters, informal influences appeared. One was a tendency to allow an exceptionally popular actress to have good roles, whether or not she was particularly well suited to the part. In Pepys' opinion this was true of the casting of Nell Gwyn, who, to his disapproval, was assigned to a serious role in *The Indian Emperour*, a tragic part which lay beyond her powers. He emphasized this view by pointing out, after seeing her and Hart perform comic roles

301 *Apology*, I, 113–14.
302 *Ibid.*, I, 113.

"most excellently" in *The Mad Couple* on 28 December 1667, that he considered "it a miracle to me to think how ill she do a serious part, as the other day, just like a fool or changeling; and, in a mad part, do beyond all imitation almost." Her current popularity undoubtedly led the managers to bring her on stage nearly every day, if possible, even at the expense of proper casting.

Another factor was the influence of outsiders, such as the King, the public, the dramatist, or the proprietor. Just as Charles II occasionally assisted a playwright in the composing of a drama, he sometimes intervened in the casting. On 8 May 1663, when Pepys attended a performance of *The Humorous Lieutenant*, he particularly noted that Lacy acted "by the King's command" the "very part" [the Lieutenant] which Walter Clun had previously played. Occasionally the proprietor, for reasons not appropriate to good casting, altered traditional assignments. In the early 1690's the ambitions of the young actors coupled with the determination of the new proprietors (Christopher Rich and Sir Thomas Skipwith) to demean the older players resulted in Thomas Betterton's being deposed from some of his customary roles in favor of a younger man, George Powell. An inner struggle for power and position, rather than the superior merit of Powell, determined the casting. The taste of the public also determined some assignments. The great popularity of Nell Gwyn and the wisdom of having an Epilogue spoken by a charming actress who could entice the audience into applause brought her many assignments of this kind. Similarly, the skill of Joseph Haines as a declamatory as well as a comic speaker created a demand for him to offer his specialties, such as an Epilogue Spoken on or beside an Ass.

The dramatist also had a hand in the casting of some plays. This procedure was probably of greatest influence when the playwright had fashioned a character with a particular performer in mind. Nahum Tate attempted to have James Nokes play a major role in *Cuckold's Haven*, ca. July 1685, but was disappointed by his unavailability, Tate emphasizing that it was Nokes "for whom it was design'd, and only proper." An outstanding example is William Congreve, whose heroines were created to the image of Anne Bracegirdle, such as Millamant in *The Way of the World*. Cibber, doubling as author and actor, stated that he "gave [himself] the Part of Sir Novelty" in his *Love's Last Shift*, January 1696, and a year later, for his second play, *Woman's Wit*, he designed Master Johnny for Dogget and assigned himself the minor role of Longville.

Another factor was a tradition of type casting. Thomas Betterton, a man of great dignity and lofty demeanor as well as fine talent, played many heroic and serious parts, such as Hamlet and The Bondman. Pepys occasionally emphasized that he had seen few roles so finely cast and acted as the Bondman played by Betterton. Similarly, Charles Hart was excellent in kingly or heroic roles (Brutus in *Julius Caesar* or Alexander in *The Rival Queens*) and Downes reported that whenever Hart appeared in his best roles even so often as once in a fortnight, "the House was fill'd as at a New Play"; furthermore, he displayed "Grandeur and Agreeable Majesty" so well "That one of the Court was pleas'd to Honour him with this Commendation: That Hart might Teach any King on Earth how to Comport himself."[303] At the other extreme, Samuel Sandford, whose physical attributes gave him a grotesque air, was often cast in villainous roles, although, as Professor Robert Ross has pointed out, this sphere was not his sole talent.[304] Cibber became excellent as a fop. Penkethman was adept at clownish, broad parts. Elizabeth Barry excelled in tragic roles. Anne Bracegirdle was distinguished as the young heroine in a comedy of manners. Naturally these factors affected the casting of new plays.

Inexperienced actors, of course, were assigned to relatively unimportant roles. Downes recalled that when he made his debut in *The Siege of Rhodes* he was so frightened at the presence of the Court that he abandoned acting to be a prompter. Thomas Otway, wishing to act, had the role of the King in *The Jealous Bridegroom* allotted him by its author, Aphra Behn, only to find that "the full House put him in such a Sweat and Tremendous Agony, being dash't, spoilt him for an Actor."[305] An examination of the casts entered in the Calendar chronologically will show how many performers made their first appearance in minor roles and rose steadily as opportunities to display their mature talents came to them.

In a repertory system, like that in operation during the period of the Restoration, rehearsing was almost continuous. Not only did the companies have to prepare new plays, but they always must be reviewing, re-casting, and refreshing the "stage business" and lines for each revived play. From the available evidence, it appears likely that the companies held formal rehearsals in the morning and mid-day and that conning lines and preparing scenes, songs, dances, and other components of the performance continued after the audience had left the theatre in the late afternoon. Actors also took their lines to their homes for study in the evening. Some of this division of labor is clarified by references to the preparations for performances. In *The*

303 *Roscius Anglicanus*, p. 16.
304 "Samuel Sandford: Villain from Necessity," pp. 367–72.
305 Downes, *Roscius Anglicanus*, p. 34.

Rehearsal (7 December 1671) remarks in the play indicate that rehearsing occurred during the morning and, as the performance did not begin until mid-afternoon, sometimes continued into the early afternoon. On the morning of 8 April 1667 Pepys wanted to see Mrs Knepp and went "to enquire out Mrs Knipp's new lodging, but could not, but do hear of her at the Play-house, where she was practicing." On 5 October 1667 he arrived at the theatre shortly after noon and discovered Mrs Knepp going over her lines for the play she was to act in that afternoon: "and here I read the questions to Knepp, while she answered me, through all her part of 'Flora's Figary's' which was acted to-day." Earlier than year Pepys gave us a glimpse of the post-performance preparations for the next day: "Knipp made us stay in a box and see the dancing preparatory to to-morrow for 'The Goblins' . . . which was pretty." On 18 September 1668, after seeing *Henry* IV, Pepys learned that Mrs Knepp had to take home with her the lines for *The Silent Woman*, in which she had to perfect herself for a performance on the following day. For a new play there were full rehearsals attended sometimes by friends of the author or the company; Evelyn apparently attended one of these on 23 December 1662 when he went to "heare the Comedians con, & repeate" the new work by Sir Samuel Tuke, *The Adventures of Five Hours*. When Dryden's *Albion and Albanius* was in preparation, Charles II (according to the Dedication of the printed text) attended more than one rehearsal, and a contemporary reported that it was "well performed at the repetition that has been made before his Majesty at the Duchess of Portsmouth's."[306]

For how long the formal rehearsal of a new play extended is not precisely known, but a month was probably a normal period. Cibber's contract for *Woman's Wit*, 29 October 1696, called for a premiere within a month after the parts had been distributed to the players.[307] *The Relapse*, December 1696, according to the First Prologue, was "Got, Conceiv'd, and Born in six Weeks space." When a play was revived and re-cast, the rehearsing had to be done quickly. Cibber offers a detailed account of an occasion when *The Old Batchelor* was revived on a sudden, the role of Fondlewife being assigned to him.

> Accordingly the Part was put into my Hands between Eleven and Twelve that Morning, which I durst not refuse because others were as much strained in time for Study as myself. But I had this casual Advantage of most of them; that having so constantly observ'd Dogget's Performance, I wanted but little Trouble to make me perfect in the Words; so that when it came to my turn to rehearse, while others read

306 1 January 1684/5. HMC, Twelfth Report, Appendix, Part 5, Rutland MSS, II, 85.
307 L. C. 7/3, in Nicoll, *Restoration Drama*, pp. 381–87.

their Parts from their Books, I had put mine in my Pocket, and went thro' the first Scenes without it; and though I was more abash'd to rehearse so remarkable a Part before the Actors (which is natural to most People) than to act before an Audience, yet some of the better-natur'd encourag'd me.[308]

During the preparation and rehearsal of a play, other problems arose. Often a drama had to be considerably altered to make it conform to pre-vailing concepts, as when Southerne and Dryden made considerable re-adjustments in Congreve's *The Old Batchelor*. Shadwell complained of the alterations which had to be made in *The Humorists*, eventually performed in December 1670: "I was forc'd, after I had finish'd it, to blot out the main design of it; finding that, contrary to my intention, it had given offence." Commenting upon the preparation of *Don Sebastian*, 4 December 1689, Dryden stated: "Above twelve hundred Lines have been cut off from this tragedy since it was first delivered to the actors." Sometimes everything seemed to go wrong. A celebrated case was David Crauford's difficulties with *Courtship a la mode*, which he submitted to Betterton's company probably early in 1700. His Preface reports in detail his misfortunes. He had no complaint against Betterton but lamented that the company failed to follow Betterton's good example. John Bowman had "the first Character of my Play six weeks, and then cou'd hardly read six lines on't." Although some members of the company "who valu'd their reputations more" rarely absented them-selves from rehearsals, many, including Bowman, did not attend at all, and Crauford observed that "six or seven people cou'd not perform what was design'd for fifteen." Withdrawing his play from Betterton's custody, he took it to Drury Lane, where it was "immediately cast to the best Advantage, and Plaid in less than twenty days." Because authors were notoriously touchy concerning the treatment of their plays, one must discount some of the complaints, yet Crauford and others argued that Betterton's company had at this time fallen into careless ways.

In fact, if one believes the outcries of many Restoration playwrights, the rehearsals were never sufficiently long or careful. At the première of Etherege's *She Would if She Could*, 6 February 1667/8, Pepys happily sat among the wits and reported that Etherege grumbled at the players: "Here was the Duke of Buckingham to-day openly sat in the pit, and there I found him with my Lord Buckhurst, and Sidly, and Etherige, the poet: the last of whom I did hear mightily find fault with the actors, that they were out of humour, and had not their parts perfect, and that Harris did do nothing, nor could so

[308] *Apology*, I, 207.

much as sing a ketch in it." In July 1677, when production facilities were not at their best, at the first performance of *The Constant Nymph* the author complained (see the Dedication) that large portions were omitted and that scarcely a single speech went unmangled; in addition, the company had spent little time or money on habits, music, and scenes.

The preparation might be faulty in other ways. Few better examples exist than the failure of the director to foresee weaknesses in the presentation of Orrery's *The Black Prince*, 19 October 1667. Present at the première, Pepys, as well as others, thought that the device of reading a long letter in it failed of its purpose.

[The] whole house was mightily pleased with it all along till towards the end he comes to discover the chief of the plot of the play by the reading of a long letter, which was so long and some things (the people being set already to think too long) so unnecessary that they frequently begun to laugh, and to hiss twenty times, that, had it not been for the King's being there, they had certainly hissed it off the stage. But I must confess that, as my Lord Barkeley says behind me, the having of that long letter was a thing so absurd, that he could not imagine how a man of his parts could possibly fall into it; or, if he did, if he had but let any friend read it, the friend would have told him of it; . . . for nothing could be more ridiculous than this, though the letter of itself at another time would be thought an excellent letter, and indeed an excellent Romance, but at the end of the play, when every body was weary of sitting, and were already possessed with the effect of the whole letter, to trouble them with a letter a quarter of an hour long, was a most absurd thing.

When Pepys next saw the drama, on 23 October 1667, the letter had been printed and circulated among the audience and cut from the play.

These were not the only problems involved in the rehearsal and production of plays. In January 1692 a dispute arose over the order of new works to be staged. Shadwell, writing on 19 January 1691/2, to the Earl of Dorset, complained that *The Innocent Impostors* had been shunted aside, apparently to favor plays by D'Urfey and Dryden. Shadwell asked that Dorset intervene and order that *The Innocent Impostors* be given priority. At times, too, the management showed poor judgment in bringing on an excessively large number of new plays so close together that none was well staged and many were, as *A Comparison Between the Two Stages* (1702) liked to state, "Damn'd." In the early winter of 1690 so many new plays were brought on in a short period that they stumbled over one another in getting onto the stage and being hustled off as failures.

THE PREMIÈRE

CHOICE OF DAY. During the opening decade of the Restoration of Charles II, no single day of the week appears to have been so eminently satisfactory for a first performance of a new play or for an auspicious revival as to indicate a decisive preference. During this decade there is, however, more evidence concerning the exact date of premières than in later years. A canvass of some thirty plays whose first performance can be dated with reasonable certainty during the ten seasons from 1660–61 through 1669–70 suggests, nevertheless, that preference rather than chance dictated the choice. Thursdays and Saturdays ranked equally high, and the only other day on which a considerable number of first performances occurred was Monday. The remaining acting days had so few premières that management apparently slighted them. With respect to revivals, the matter is complicated by the fact that for a while nearly every play acted represents a revival. In addition, less fanfare was attached to a revival and Pepys does not always indicate when an old play has just reappeared in the repertory. Nevertheless, for some fifteen plays whose revival can be clearly assigned to a particular day, Saturday leads the list, with Friday and Thursday only slightly less favored.

As one looks at both new plays and revivals, Saturday appears to have been the preferred day, Thursday slightly less so. No contemporary discussion of this problem exists. One may speculate that a première on Saturday offered the advantage of a full week of rehearsals and an opportunity to polish the production for a second performance after a Sunday without performances. So little evidence concerning the dates on which premières fell in the last three decades of the century that they offer little assistance with this problem.

ATMOSPHERE. Of all the theatrical events in Restoration London, none was more colorful than the first performance of a new play. For many days before the opening the town had heard intimations of what was being prepared, and Pepys' pressing desire to attend premières testifies to the enticement which they offered. The wits, theatrically knowledgeable Londoners, the author and his friends (as well as his enemies) gathered to see how well the staged play matched the word-of-mouth account which had circulated through London. Many authors as well as many observers have left records of the exciting and sometimes exasperating incidents associated with the première.

In the first place, the lack of a satisfactory system of reserving places made the afternoon a confusing, even a frustrating effort for the spectators. On several occasions Pepys, warned by experience, went early, but so did many others, as it was, basically, first come, first served, with the exception of royalty and other persons of influence who had places held for them. On 19 October 1667, when Orrery's *The Black Prince* was on the bill as a new play, Pepys found that "though we come by two o'clock, yet there was no room in the pit." On 6 February 1667/8, when *She Would if She Could* was first presented, the press was greater: "though I was there by two o'clock, there was 1000 people put back that could not have room in the pit." On 26 March 1667/8 he arrived even earlier to see Davenant's *The Man's the Master*, "where the house was, it being not above twelve o'clock, very full." On 2 May 1668 for the première of *The Sullen Lovers*, he arrived at "a little past twelve," three hours before curtain time. Obviously word of mouth brought out the "knowing" part of the town. As the Prologue to *The Comical Revenge*, March 1663/4, put it with a satiric touch:

> *Who cou'd expect such crowding here to day,*
> *Meerly on the report of a new play?*

As a result of these and other complications, the first day was not always conducive to a proper atmosphere for appreciating a new work. Pepy attended *The Adventures of Five Hours* on 8 January 1662/3 and was "forced to sit almost out of sight, at the end of one of the lower forms, so full was the house." At *The Change of Crowns*, 15 April 1667, he had "to stand all the whole close to the very door till I took cold." Sometimes delays marred the occasion. Whenever royalty attended, the program could not begin until the King had arrived, and the royal party often was in no hurry. At *The Sullen Lovers*, 2 May 1668, Pepys arrived at noon and found the wait tiring until "by and by the King comes and the Duke of York; and then the play begins." On 23 February 1668/9, arriving before one o'clock and, with others in a house "infinite full," he had to wait until "by and by the King and Court come."

In addition, acting on the first day was often less than adequate. Attending a new revival of *Romeo and Juliet*, 1 March 1661/2, Pepys, disappointed, "resolved to go no more to see the first time of acting, for they were all of them out more or less." Mention has already been made of the dismal acting by John Downes, making his debut in *The Siege of Rhodes*, and by Thomas Otway, playing his first role as the King in *The Forc'd Marriage*. The Preface to Dilke's *The City Lady*, ca. December 1696, paints a picture of an unhappy premiere.

The tedious waiting to have the Curtain drawn, after the Prologue was spoke, occasion'd by Mr Underhill's violent Bleeding, put the Audience out of Humour, and made it susceptible of the least Disgust; and when once the Torrent of its Displeasure break bounds, nothing cou'd put a stop to its Vehemence. After Mr Underhill was no longer able to come upon the Stage, scarce any thing was done but by Halves, and in much Confusion.

Edward Howard, commenting upon the initial showing of his *Women's Conquest*, ca. November 1670, complained of its "having some of the Parts ill and imperfectly performed." In the Dedication to *The Siege of Memphis*, ca. September 1676, the author regretted "the ill representation at the Theatre, being play'd to the worst advantage." At *The Wary Widow*, ca. March 1693, the actors were "completely drunk" by the end of Act III and unable to complete the performance.[309] And surely one of the memorable first performances was that of *The Relapse*, 21 November 1696, when Jack Verbruggen, acting Loveless, had imbibed so freely before and during the drinking scenes on stage that he came near to a literal assault instead of the simulated seduction in the script.

The plight of the dramatist, especially at a première, became, in fact, a subject for mild or caustic satire among spectators, actors, and fellow playwrights. In the Preface to *The Sullen Lovers*, 2 May 1668, Shadwell looked wryly at all modern authors "such as peep through their loop-holes in the Theatre, to see who looks grim upon their Playes: And if they spy a Gentle Squire making Faces, he poor soul must be Hector'd till he likes 'em." Earlier the Prologue to Porter's *The Villain*, 18 October 1663, had begged pity for the uneasy dramatist.

> But (*Gentlemen*) in troth I'm only come
> To tell ye that the Author is gone home,
> To shun your Doom, like some poor Couzen'd Wench
> That had not Confidence t'out-face the Bench.
> We were such Fools as to perswade his Stay,
> But (smiling at us) He made haste away.

Somberly the playwright might be present, as the Prologue by Dryden to *The Pilgrim* stated, to see his rivals in composition hissing and damning his play.

> Their Brother Poets Damn the Play
> And Roar the loudest, tho' they never pay.[310]

---

309 Charles Gildon, *The Life of Mr Thomas Betterton* (London, 1710), p. 20.

310 The Prologue refers, in the last phrase, to the fact that dramatists often received free admittance to the theatre for a few months after a première, a privilege which the author of *A Comparison Between the Two Stages* ridiculed as one which led some amateurs to aspire to dramatic composition.

In spite of the confusion, disturbances, and uneasiness sometimes prevailing at the first performance, the judgment of able men could insure a favorable verdict. John Dennis, writing years after the event, gave a dramatic version of how Wycherley's *The Plain Dealer* fared on 11 December 1676.

The Town . . . appeared Doubtful what Judgment to Form of it . . . [the Duke of Buckingham, Earl of Rochester, Earl of Dorset, Earl of Mulgrave, Savil, Buckly, Sit John Denham and Edmund Waller] by their loud approbation of it, gave it both a sudden and a lasting reputation.[311]

THE RUN

In the modern sense of the word, the "run" was not a major element in the professional theatre, primarily because the repertory system depended upon a constant rotation of old plays with an intermingling of new ones. The repertory was a reservoir from which the company drew its constant flow of plays, the reservoir being replenished from time to time by an infusion of new works. With a relatively limited potential audience, the initial run was sustained by the spectators who wished to see it for the first time and who were drawn back for a second or third performance. (Pepys occasionally attended a new play two or three times within its first week.) In addition, the dramatist had a financial interest only in a short run, for he had a benefit on the third day, sometimes on the sixth; but until the ninth day became established as an additional benefit, he had only the prestige of an extended run to make him press for continuance.

In the first ten years following 1660, Downes, prompter for the Duke's Company, frequently indicated the relative success of new or revived plays by listing the number of consecutive performances. Davenant's *The Wits* (15 August 1661) was acted eight days successively; *The Adventures of Five Hours* (8 January 1662/3), thirteen days; a revival of *The Humorous Lieutenant* at the opening of the new theatre in Drury Lane (8 May 1663), twelve performances. Runs of ten to fifteen performances between 1660 and 1670 represented unusually successful productions: a revival of *Henry* VIII (22 December 1663) "15 Days together with general Applause"; *Tyrannic Love* (24 June 1669) and *The Woman Made a Justice* (19 February 1669/70) had runs of fourteen consecutive days.[312]

311 *The Works of John Dennis*, II, 277.
312 *Roscius Anglicanus*, pp. 21, 23, 24.

In the later years a few plays had even greater success, with emphasis upon a large number of performances during the first season rather than a spectacular initial run. *A Citizen Turned Gentleman* (4 July 1672) had a first run of nine days, but the Preface implies that it was acted about thirty times in a short period. At the end of the century Farquhar's *The Constant Couple* (29 November 1699) had an enormous success, the Preface stating that it "brought the Play-house some fifty Audiences in five Months." On the other hand, Downes significantly emphasized that some new plays barely managed a run of six days, others but three in a row. He pointed out that Settle's *Cambyses* (10 January 1670/1) "Succeeded six Days with a full Audience"; *The Gentleman Dancing Master* (6 February 1671/2) lasted "but 6 Days"; *The History of Charles* VIII *of France* (18 November 1671) "but 6 Days together."[313] Sometimes a play went slightly beyond the sixth day (a mark of moderate success) but then faltered: *Lover's Luck* (December 1695) filled the house for six days and brought an audience paying £50 on the eighth day, its last sequential performance.[314] On the other hand, Dilke's *The City Lady* (December 1696), according to the Preface, lasted three days only. Few plays seem to have collapsed completely on the first day, for the author's friends often rallied to make certain that he had the third day's benefit. In fact, the importance of the run was two-fold. It reimbursed the company for the expense of a new production and indicated whether the play might be worth reviving later; and it enabled the author to secure a financial reward from his composition. The same considerations remained effective into the following century.

[313] *Ibid.*, pp. 27, 32.
[314] *Ibid.*, p. 44.

The Audience

COMPOSITION

The common assumption is that the Restoration audience was essentially of upper-class composition by contrast with the greater diversity of classes, education, and taste of the Elizabethan era. Nevertheless, the Restoration audience was not of the single complexion which some subsequent theatrical historians have emphasized. The range of social classes, professions, and cultural attainments was fairly great, and the taste of the spectators as well as their motives in attending the playhouses varied considerably. Some, like Pepys, were fascinated by the stage, by the sense of illusion, and by the social structure of the spectators. Others, like James Brydges, in the closing decade, apparently regarded the theatre as a port of call on the social round, where Brydges might look in and quickly withdraw if the atmosphere did not attract him. Many men of letters attended frequently, sometimes as arbiters of taste, sometimes because the theatre was, except for the Court, the coffee-houses, and private homes, a center where intellectuals met and kept abreast of literary tendencies, the old and new drama, and the climate of acting. To it also came many wits, gentlemen, Persons of Quality, citizens, Templars, and other of varying social and financial status.

In fact, the audience seems to have been of almost unceasing interest to itself, to playwrights, to authors of prologues and epilogues, and to pamphleteers. They tended to categorize the spectators and to define their habitats. Pepys, an observant man, often responded to the composition of the audience, partly because he was delighted when interesting wits and lovely ladies attended, and disappointed when lower social groups dominated. He also enjoyed a play more when there was a full house, for a meager one had a desolate air. In fact, the social atmosphere of the theatre was rarely better captured than by Pepys, attending *Heraclius* on 4 February 1666/7; he had

[an] extraordinary content; and the more from the house being very full, and great company; among others, Mrs Steward, very fine, with her locks done up with puffs . . . and several other great ladies, had their hair so. . . . Here I saw my Lord Rochester

and his lady, Mrs Mallet, who hath after all this ado married him; and, as I hear some say in the pit, it is a great act of charity; for he hath no estate. But it was pleasant to see how everybody rose up when my Lord John Butler, the Duke of Ormond's son, come into the pit towards the end of the play, who was a servant to Mrs Mallet, and now smiled upon her, and she on him. I had sitting next to me a woman, the likest my Lady Castlemayne that ever I saw anybody like another; but she is a whore, I believe, for she is acquainted with every fine fellow, and called them by their name, Jacke, and Tom, and before the end of the play frisked to another place.

How like a social afternoon, lacking only tea to make the gossipy atmosphere complete. In other vignettes Pepys suggests the informality of the auditors. On 16 September 1667 he recorded that "one of the best parts of our sport was a mighty pretty lady that sat behind us, that did laugh so heartily and constantly, that it did me good to hear her." Or a touchingly sentimental scene, at *The Mad Couple*, 28 December 1667: "It pleased us mightily to see the natural affection of a poor woman, the mother of one of the children brought upon the stage: the child crying, she by force got upon the stage and took up her child and carried it away off of the stage from Hart [the actor]." Or a moment of near tragedy, averted skillfully, on 2 November 1667 at *1 Henry* IV: "And it was observable how a gentleman of good habit, sitting just before us, eating of some fruit in the midst of the play, did drop down as dead, being choked; but with much ado Orange Moll did thrust her finger down his throat, and brought him to life again."

   Some contemporary writers attempted to understand the composition and alteration in the audiences during the forty years preceding 1700; usually, they made distinctions between the spectators during the reign of Charles II and those from the accession of William and Mary to the end of the century. The author of *Historia Histrionica* (1699) briefly examined conditions before the Civil Wars, during the Commonwealth, and after the Restoration. In his opinion, although London was much more populous after 1660 than before the Commonwealth, the increase in admission charges in the Restoration playhouses (which he blames upon the introduction of costly scenes) narrowed the range of individuals who could afford to attend. As a result, there was "better order kept among the Company that came; which made very good People think a Play an Innocent Diversion for an idle Hour or two." In addition, he believed that the plays after 1660 were, "for the most part, more Instructive and Moral."[315] From a vantage point in the early eighteenth century, John Dennis also looked back upon the reign

---

[315] In Cibber, *Apology*, I, xxvii.

of Charles II and analyzed the nature of the audience at that time. First of all, he believed that "a considerable Part" of the auditory "had that due application, which is requisite for the judging of Comedy," the leisure to attend to dramatic theory and practice, for "that was an age of Pleasure, and not of Business." Gentlemen had the financial security and leisure to be "serene enough to receive its impressions."316 Later, Dennis returned to this subject and emphasized another factor which he thought made the audiences of the reign of Charles II superior: There "were several extraordinary men at Court who wanted neither Zeal nor Capacity, nor Authority to sett [the audiences] right again." He named, among others, George Villiers Duke of Buckingham, John Wilmot Earl of Rochester, the Earl of Dorset, Sir John Denham, and Edmund Waller. Men of their culture, knowledge, and taste could strongly influence an audience. When "these or the Majority of them Declared themselves upon any new Dramatick performance, the Town fell Immediately in with them."317

An examination of the known records of attendance at the theatres between 1660 and 1670 will document some of the analysis which Dennis made. The diaries and correspondence for that period show that a considerable number of literary men attended the theatre, some with considerable frequency: Sir Charles Sedley, Sir George Etherege, the Earl of Dorset, George Villiers Duke of Buckingham, Thomas Shadwell, John Dryden, Roger Boyle Earl of Burlington, Sir William Coventry, the Earl of Rochester, William Cavendish Duke of Newcastle, Thomas Killigrew, Sir William Davenant. No doubt, many of the dramatists attended the opening performances of their own plays and, probably, those of rival playwrights. Pepys also gave particular attention to the nobility, gentlemen, and ladies attending the theatre. He noted that Charles II attended frequently, sometimes accompanied by the Duke and Duchess of York, often with other nobles and Ladies of Honour; in addition, the Lord Chamberlain's records list many other occasions on which royalty was present. When Elizabeth, Queen of Bohemia visited in London, she also attended the theatres. Other frequenters during this period were Lord Brouncker and Sir William Penn, both close friends to Pepys; he often accompanied other members of the Penn family. Among other upper-class auditors were: Sir Christopher North, Sir Philip Carteret, John Evelyn, Prince Rupert, Lord Lauderdale, the Duke of Ormond, Lord Arlington, the Duke of Norfolk, the Duke of Albemarle, Lord Sandwich,

316 *Works*, I, 293-94.
317 *Ibid.*, II, 277. At this point he offered as an influence their verdict on *The Plain Dealer*, referred to earlier, which turned the opinion of the town in its favor.

Sir William Batten, Dr Thomas Sprat, Bishop of Rochester, Lord Faucon-berg, Henry Savile.

Pepys also frequently recorded in his Diary the presence of "fine ladies." He was particularly aware of Lady Castlemayne's presence in the playhouse and occasionally, seeing her carriage outside the theatre, could hardly resist the temptation to go into the playhouse in spite of a resolve not do so. He noticed also that the actresses from one company attended the opposition offerings whenever practicable, seeing Mrs Knepp and Betty Hall of the King's Company at the Duke's Theatre on 30 March 1667. Nell Gwyn and Hester Davenport were sometimes conspicuously present, Mrs Davenport sitting in the box at *The Villain* on 1 January 1662/3 and catching Pepys' eye. Later, as we know from the Lord Chamberlain's records, Nell Gwyn attended the theatres frequently on the King's bounty. Lady Dorset, Lady Penn, Lady Elizabeth Bodvile, Mlle Le Blanc, Queen Elizabeth of Bohemia and other ladies of fashion filled the boxes.

Attending as regularly as his conscience and purse would allow, Pepys makes it clear that some of his friends were equally attentive playgoers. Captain Ferrers and John Creed, a Deputy-Treasurer to the Fleet, often were Pepys' companions on a playgoing afternoon. On other occasions he attended with the Penn family, sometimes with Lord Brouncker, or with ladies of the circles in which Pepys moved. He refers occasionally to the presence of "gallants," sometimes as though they were a disturbing breed but rarely naming them. Much of what Pepys reports bears out Thomas Killigrew's assertions, 12 February 1666/7, concerning the improved atmos-phere at the King's Theatre: earlier "the Queen seldom and the King never would come; now, not the King only for state, but all civil people do think they may come as well as any." In addition, Killigrew "tells me plainly that the City audience was as good as the Court, but now they are most gone."

Nevertheless, Pepys makes us aware that a greater diversity of persons by class, birth, and occupation attended occasionally and, apparently, with greater frequency year by year. On 27 December 1662 he was "not so well pleased with the company at the house to-day, which was full of citizens, there hardly being a gentleman or woman in the house." On 1 January 1662/3 he reported: "The house was full of citizens, and so the less pleasant." Attending *Tu Quoque*, 12 September 1667, he disliked the play, adding, "but it will please the citizens." At *1 Henry* IV, 2 November 1667, he especially noted that "The house [was] full of Parliamentmen," as a result of a holiday for them. In a thoughtful mood on 1 January 1667/8 at *The Feigned Innocence*, he reflected on the changes he had seen in several years of theatregoing:

"Here a mighty company of citizens, 'prentices, and others; and it makes me observe, that when I begun first to be able to bestow a play on myself, I do not remember that I saw so many by half of the ordinary 'prentices and mean people in the pit at 2s. 6d. a-piece as now."

If we turn to the last twenty years of the seventeenth century, the evidence suggests that changes had occurred in the composition of the audience. Dennis believed that the quality and taste of the spectators had seriously declined by 1700. Commenting upon the audiences of 1702, he found there "three sorts of People . . . who have had no education at all; and who were unheard of in the Reign of Charles the Second." These included (a) a "great many younger Brothers, Gentlemen born, who had been kept at home, by reason of the pressure of the Taxes"; (b) individuals "who made their Fortunes in the late War" and who had risen "from a state of obscurity" to a "condition of distinction and plenty"; and (c) "that considerable number of Foreigners, which within the last twenty years have been introduc'd among us; some of whom not being acquainted with our Language, and consequently with the sense of our Plays, and others disgusted with our extravagant, exorbitant Rambles, have been Instrumental in introducing Sound and Show." The second group, in his view, "could never attain to any higher entertainment than Tumbling and Vaulting and Ladder Dancing, and the delightful diversions of Jack Pudding . . . and encourage these noble Pastimes still upon the Stage." The third group, furthermore, like "Sound and Show, where the business of the Theatre does not require it, and particularly a sort of soft and wanton Musick, which has used the People to a delight which is independent of Reason, a delight that has gone a very great way towards the enervating and dissolving their minds." Finally, he argued that by 1702 "there are ten times more Gentlemen now in business, than there were in King Charles his Reign." They have been disturbed by war and pressed by taxes, "which make them uneasie." As a result, they "are attentive in the events of affairs, and too full of great and real events, to receive due impressions from the imaginary ones of the Theatre."[318] In a somewhat similar vein the author of *Historia Histrionica* (1699) emphasized that in the late years of the seventeenth century "The Play-houses are so

---

[318] *Ibid.*, I, 293–94. One cannot help being reminded, at this point, of the way in which Pepys, concerned with the affairs of the navy and the state, nevertheless responded to the illusion of the stage. On 5 October 1667, dropping behind the scenes at Bridges Street, he expressed this sense of illusion: "But, Lord! to see how they [Mrs Knepp and Nell Gwyn] were both painted would make a man mad, and did make me loath them; and what base company of men comes among them, and how lewdly they talk! and how poor the men are in clothes, and yet what a shew they make on the stage by candle-light, is very observable."

extreamly pestered with Vizard-masks and their Trade (occasioning continual Quarrels and Abuses) that many of the more Civilized Part of the Town are uneasy in the Company, and shun the Theatre as they would a House of Scandal."319

An associated influence was a change in the management. In the fifteen years following 1660 management lay in the hands of individuals who, frequently, were both proprietors and dramatists (Sir William Davenant is an example), and the actor-sharers had an interest in attracting audiences who responded to the best in dramatic offerings. After 1682, and especially in the last decade, when Rich and Skipwith bought into the United Company, they catered to a diversified audience. In part, they responded to a change; in part, they broadened the range of spectators and tastes.

The writers of Prologues and Epilogues and of pamphlets also show the diversified nature of the audience, especially from 1670 to 1700. They tend also to characterize the spectators in each section of the house, from the boxes to the upper gallery. In a Prologue spoken after the King's Company had suffered a fire at Drury Lane in 1672, Dryden presented a panoramic view of the audience.

> *Here's good Accommodation in the Pit,*
> *The Grave demurely in the midst may Sit.*
> *And so the hot Burgundians on the Side,*
> *Ply Vizard Masque, and o're the Benches stride:*
> *Here are convenient upper boxes too,*
> *For those that make the most trimphant show,*
> *All that keep Coaches must not Sit below.*
> *There Gallants, You betwixt the Acts retire,*
> *And at dull Plays have something to admire.*

Examining the habituees of the pit, some writers look at them caustically, some gently. In *The Young Gallant's Academy* (1674) the satirist pictures the young man who attends the play to draw attention to himself.

Therefore, I say, let our Gallant . . . presently advance himself into the middle of the Pit, where having made his Honor to the rest of the Company, but especially to the Vizard-Masks, let him pull out his comb, and manage his flaxen Wig with all the Grace he can. Having so done, the next step is to give a hum to the China-Orange-Wench, and give her her own rate for her Oranges (for 'tis beneath a Gentleman to stand haggling like a Citizens wife) and then to present the fairest to the next Vizard-mask. And that I may incourage our Gallant not like the Tradesman to save a shilling,

319 In Cibber, *Apology*, I, xxvii.

and so sit but in the Middle-Gallery, let him but consider what large comings-in are pursued up sitting in the Pit.

The Gallant, the satirist continues, can thus gain a "conspicuous Eminence," and, if he is a knight, secure a mistress. In addition, "It shall frown you with rich Commendations, to laugh aloud in the midst of the most serious and sudden Scene of the terriblest Tragedy, and to let the Clapper (your Tongue) be tossed so high, that all the House may ring of it." Further, the Gallant can "publish your tempera . . . to the world, in that you seem not to resort thither to taste vain Pleasures with a hungry Appetite; but only as a Gentleman to spend a foolish hour or two, because you can do nothing else."[320]

From 1660 to 1700 the writers of prologues and epilogues emphasize the conspicuous behavior of the young-man-about-town in the pit. According to the Prologue to *The Comical Revenge*, March 1664:

> *And Gallants, as for you, talk loud i'th' Pit,*
> *Divert your selves and Friends with your own Wit.*

More caustic is the Prologue to *The Ordinary*, ca. January 1670/1.

> *Some come with lusty Burgundy half-drunk,*
> *T'eat China Oranges, make love to Punk;*
> *And briskly mount a bench when th' Act is done,*
> *And comb their much-lov'd Periwigs to the tune*
> *And can sit out a Play of three hours long,*
> *Minding no part of 't but the Dance or Song.*

That for *The Rival Queens*, 17 March 1676/7, ridicules the gallants who "with loud Nonsense drown the Stages Wit," a point reiterated in the Epilogue to *Sertorius*, ca. March 1679: "[Our Poet] scorns those little Vermin in the Pit, / Who noise and nonsense vent insteat of Wit."[321] They tended to put on a show of their own (Epilogue to Mrs Behn's *The False Count*):

> *You Sparks better Comedians are than we;*
> *You every day out-fool ev'n Nokes and Lee.*
> *They're forc'd to stop, and their own Farces quit,*
> *T'admire the Merry-Andrews of the Pit.*

Although many commentators lashed the gallants and fops in the Pit, the boxes commonly held more sedate and, theoretically, more sympathetic

---

[320] Pp. 56–58.
[321] The Prologue to *Bellamira*, 12 May 1687, also criticized the excessive noise in the Pit: "Tho the shrill Pit be louder than the Stage."

spectators. Here frequently sat the Ladies to whom the writers of Epilogues turned with requests that the warm-hearted "Fair Sex" lead the spectators to a favorable verdict. Here, too, sat the upper classes, a fact which attracted Pepys on 1 May 1667: "We sat at the upper bench next the boxes; and I find it do pretty well, and have the advantage of seeing and hearing the great people." Even Robert Gould's caustic satire, *The Play-House* (1685), acknowledged the gentility of the boxes: "And for the Muse a Nobler Scene prepare, / And let Her breathe in Milder air." Even so, the side-boxes irritated commentators by inattentiveness to the play and by devotion to flirtation. As Lord Foppington in *The Relapse*, December 1696, remarked: "But a Man must endeavour to look wholesome, lest he makes so nauseous a Figure in the Side-box, the Ladies shou'd be compell'd to turn their Eyes upon the Play."

For the Galleries, however, the commentators often saved their sharpest barbs. Just as the fops sometimes turned to the side-boxes for intrigue, so they, as the Prologue to Shadwell's *Woman Captain*, September 1679, states, "Whom mounting from the Pit we use to see / (For dangerous Intrigues) to th'Gallery." In the Epilogue to the opening of the theatre, 16 November 1682, Dryden vividly re-created the scene.

> *Methinks some Vizard Masque I see,*
> *Cast but her Lure from the mid Gallery.*
> *About her all the flutt'ring Sparks are rang'd;*
> *The Noise continues though the Scene is chang'd:*
> *Now growling, sputtring, wauling, such a clutter.*
> . . . .
> *Then for your Lacqueys, and your Train beside,*
> *(By what e'er Name or Title dignify'd)*
> *They roar so loud, you'd think behind the Stairs*
> *Tom Dove, and all the Brotherhood of Bears:*
> *They're grown a Nuisance, beyond all Disasters,*
> *We've none so great but their unpaying Masters.*
> *We beg you, Sirs, to beg your Men, that they*
> *Wou'd please to give you leave to hear the Play.*[322]

The Prologue to Southerne's *The Disappointment*, 5 April 1684, spoke still more sharply.

> *Last, some there are, who take their first Degrees*
> *Of Lewdness in our Middle Galleries:*

[322] The problem of footmen in the galleries was to become a serious one in the eighteenth century.

> The Doughty Bullies enter Bloody Drunk,
> Invade and grabble one another's Punk:
> They Caterwoul, and make a dismal Rout,
> Call Sons of Whores, and strike, but ne're lugg-out.

The Playhouse (1685), consistently caustic, was most severe in castigating the galleries.

> The Middle Galle'ry first demands our View;
> The filth of Jakes, and stench of ev'ry Stew!
> Here reeking Punks like Ev'ning Insects swarm;
> The Polecat's Perfume much the Happier Charm.
> Their very Scent gives Apoplectick Fits,
> And yet they're thought all Civit by the Cits;
> Nor can we blame 'em; for the Truth to tell,
> The want of Brains may be the Want of Smell.
> Here ev'ry Night they sit three Hours for Sale;
> The Night-rail always cleanlier than the Tayl.

If one believed the exaggeration of the commentators, the theatre would appear to be a place wholly inimical to the art of the drama. In fact, a disparaging view was summed up by Jovial, speaking in James Wright's *The Humours and Conversations of the Town* (1693), who replied to a question concerning the value of attending plays:

What wou'd you go to the Play for? . . . to be dun'd all round with the impertinent Discourse of Beardless Fops to the Orange-Wenches, with Commodes an Ell high; and to the Vizor-Masks: of the Rake-Hells, talking loud to one another; or the perpetual Chat of the Noisy Coquets, that come there to get Cullies, and to disturb, not mind the Play. Or to what Effect has all the Plays upon you? Are not your Fops in the Pit and Boxes incorrigible to all the Endeavours of your Writers, in their Prologues and Epilogues, or the variety of Characters that have been made to reform them? Tho a Play be an generous Diversion, yet 'tis better to read than see, unless one cou'd see it without these Inconveniences.[323]

Obviously, these views are extremist, an exaggeration of the worst elements in the theatres, for no playhouse could exist if all the audiences at all times were composed of spectators like those described in these vignettes. Nevertheless, the satirists strike at characteristics of audiences lamented by all players and playwrights: their inability to be quiet, to lend full attention to the play, and to subordinate their personal interests to the

[323] Pp. 105–6.

serious aims of author and actor, who had a good deal of right on their side. After all, quarrels and disturbances sometimes made the pit a noisy place and disrupted the play. The orangewomen bargained for their goods and charms not only in the intervals but sometimes during the action on stage. The intrigues of the gallants almost never ceased. And the gentlemen, wits, and Templars considered it their privilege to be critics, wise or witty but usually vocal. In the long run, however, the best of the drama survived and the worst died away as the judgment of the spectators surmounted temporary confusions of the moment.

CRITICISM AND JUDGMENT

The belief that the best judgment of the audience ultimately prevailed was suggested in the Prologue to *The Country Captain*, possibly revived in 1689 or 1690.

> *And 'tis the diff'rence which true Critiques make*
> *Betwixt Good Plays, and Plays which onely take,*
> *Slight flashy witt may please the present tast,*
> *But that must have a Genius which will last.*[324]

In making this judgment, the spectators claimed the right of criticism at all times. As Pepys pointed out, wits like Sir Charles Sedley commented shrewdly upon the play in progress, and Pepys was fascinated by Sedley's cleverness as well as dismayed at the interruption to his attentiveness. Looming large in the playwrights' minds were those vocal commentators categorized as the "Criticks." The most insidious, at least to the playwright, were those who came to hiss, and this group persisted from early to late. As the Prologue to *Mr Anthony*, 14 December 1669, stated:

> *He who comes hither with design to hiss,*
> *And with a Bum reverst to whisper Miss,*
> *To comb a Perriwigg, or to show gay Cloaths,*
> *Or to vent Antick nonsense with new Oaths.*

In the Prologue to Shadwell's *Epsom Wells*, 2 December 1672, the speaker plaintively asserted: "Tis not fair Play, that one for his Half Crown / Shou'd judge, and rail, and damn for half the Town." This irresponsibility was satirized in the Prologue to *A Commonwealth of Women*, August 1685.

---

[324] By Thomas Shadwell, in *A Collection of Poems by several Hands*, ed. Francis Needham, *Welbeck Miscellany, Number 2* (Bungay, Suffolk, 1934), p. 50.

Criticks, like Flyes, have several Species.
There's one that just has paid his grutch'd half Crown,
Cries, Rot the Play, Pox on't, lets cry it down.

And in Act I of *Love for Love* (30 April 1695) Scandal characterized those "huge proportion'd Criticks, with long Wigs, lac'd Coats, Steinkirk Cravats, and terrible Faces; with Cat-calls in their Hands."

It was the critic or party of hecklers who came with determination to damn the play that most perturbed the playwright. In the relatively intimate London theatrical circles, literary factions made themselves heard both inside and outside the theatre. Pepys' frequent reports of theatrical gossip show how easily news spread. In a society where Dryden and Shadwell sparred with each other—*MacFlecknoe* is an instance—or *The Rehearsal* openly ridiculed Dryden, the opposition to a new play often formed before the drama had a hearing on stage. Thomas Shadwell reported quite fully what happened to his *The Humorists*, 10 December 1670. As pointed out earlier, he had been forced to revise the "main design" of the play, but even this concession did not stifle the opposition. According to the Preface, "Notwithstanding I had . . . given satisfaction to all the exceptions made against it, it met with the clamorous opposition of a numerous party, bandied against it, and resolved, as much as they could, to damn it, right or wrong, before they had heard or seen a word on't." Similar incidents had occurred earlier, even at revivals. At *Catiline* on 18 December 1668 Katherine Corey had played Sempronia in a style to ridicule Lady Harvey. Pepys heard about it on 15 January 1668/9, when Sir William Coventry reported on the factions developing at Court from Mrs Corey's action. Later, according to Pepys, Lady Harvey "got my Lord Chamberlain, her kinsman, to imprison Doll [Mrs Corey]; when my Lady Castlemayne made the King to release her, and to order her to act it again, worse than ever the other day, where the King himself was: and since it was acted again, and my Lady Harvey provided people to hiss her and fling oranges at her." In the presence, however, of such a concentrated body of excerpts from prologues, epilogues, and satires dealing with the exuberance and misbehavior of the audience, one must constantly keep in mind the evidence in the Calendar of continuing runs of good plays and their incorporation into the repertory. The subtleties of dialogue and what may seem to our generation as endless conversations in such plays as *Aureng-Zebe*, *The Man of Mode*, *The Plain Dealer*, and *The Way of the World*, to select but a few, were listened to attentively, again, and again, and again, or they would never have crept into the repertory and

lasted as the records of their performances indicated they did. The theatre
was a business, and no manager found profit in repeating damned plays. An
examination of the Calendar will show numerous examples of plays revived
time and again to an audience which would have damned them to oblivion
had not the dramas proved themselves before a highly critical audience.

On the other hand, the favorable judgment by persons of taste or
position assisted in securing a favorable verdict. In addition to the examples
already mentioned, such as the applause aroused for Wycherley's *The Plain
Dealer*, Downes, speaking of *The Squire of Alsatia*, May 1688, stressed that it
was "often Honour'd with the presence of Chancellor Jefferies" and other
great persons who gave it applause. In the Dedication to *Theodosius*, ca.
September 1680, Nathaniel Lee expressed his gratitude to the Duchess of
Richmond for bringing Her Royal Highness "just at the exigent Times" to
secure the author's fame and a good benefit.

The judgments of the audience were, of course, influenced by differences
in taste, a point treated by Dennis in his appraisal of the quality of the
spectators throughout these forty years. Occasional remarks suggest the
kinds of elements which some in the audience enjoyed. In the Epilogue to
William Cartwright's *The Ordinary*, ca. January 1670/1, the author stated:
"The upper Gall'rie shall have their desire, / Who love a Fool, a Devil and a
Friar." In the Dedication to *The Squire of Alsatia*, May 1688, the dramatist
decried the liking of the age to "run mad after Farces," a point emphasized
also in the second part of *The Play-House* (1685). Even those not fully sympathetic with the moralists suggested that the age had an excessive enjoyment of innuendo and ribaldry. The Prologue to Aphra Behn's *The Amorous
Prince* (1671) argued:

> *Who swear they'd rather hear a smutty Jest*
> *Spoken by Nokes or Angel . . .*
> *Who love the comick Hat, the Jig and Dance.*

The author of *The Play-House* (1685) agreed: "Not only Farce; our Plays alike
are Writ / With neither Manners, Modesty, or Wit," and gave a specific
example.

> *The London Cuckolds [wives] all Flock to see,*
> *And Triumph in their Infidelity.*

Nevertheless, in the midst of these caustic views of the deplorable taste of
much of the audience, the author of *The Play-House* (1685), whose tone is
fundamentally satiric, asserted: "But if with Profit you wou'd reap Delight, /

Lay Shakespeare, Ben, and Fletcher in Your sight," for there, he argued, one will find "Natures secret Springs," art, wit, and the passions. In the highest rank of contemporary appreciation he placed *Hamlet*, *Othello*, *Timon of Athens*, *King Lear*, and *The Tempest*, although he admitted that many of these appeared in altered versions. Nevertheless, he suggested that the good Third Day's benefit which the alterer received was due chiefly to Shakespeare's merit. Similarly, he lauded appreciation of *Philaster*, *The Maid's Tragedy*, and *A King and No King*, which will never die "but reach, with like Applause, to late Posterity." Although he did not particularize the plays of "mighty Ben" Jonson, he felt that he could not pick a single work of Jonson's on which to concentrate admiration. The author concluded this portion of his praise with a summation of the best which the taste of contemporary audiences could admire:

> *Hail Sacred Bards! Hail ye Immortal Three!*
> *The British Muses, Great Triumviri!*
> *Secure of Fame, You on the Stage will live*
> *Whilst we have Wits to hear, and they have Praise to give.*[325]

Essentially, it appears that both the audience and its taste altered during these forty years. In 1660 the spectators were principally moderately cultured, well-educated persons; nevertheless, there had been an interregnum of a generation for whom the professional theatre hardly existed. During the forty years new segments of the populace had been attracted to the play-houses. Part of this change occurred through the introduction of scenes and entr'acte entertainments, the development of musical drama and spectacle, and the presence of women on the stage. In addition, it was no longer a simple case of a select audience interested principally in the drama as an art form. Management and audience had brought into being the concept of the diversified program, a concept of "good theatre" which was to prevail, to be accentuated, in the next century. A repertory theatre of the kind prevailing in the late seventeenth century, in fact, relies upon the concept of diversity in the selection of the plays to be exhibited, for it must present a balanced program of the old and new, the fresh revivals of older plays and the constant offering of the best from the past; it is only a short step to the conception of a diversified program appealing to a varied audience. Although many

---

[325] See the section on The Repertory: General View, as well as many contemporary references, comments, and allusions to the works of these authors as an indication of the way in which the repertory system preserved and revived the best in the drama and allowed the neglected older plays to be revived occasionally to see if previous judgments had been erroneous.

critics and spectators lamented this change of content and spirit, the late seventeenth century had not abrogated its responsibility to quality and good taste. It brought into being some of the most enduring English comedies of manners. The fame of some of its playwrights—John Dryden, Sir George Etherege, William Wycherley, William Congreve, Sir John Vanbrugh—is secure. It augmented the role of music within the professional theatre, and one of the great composers of the age—Henry Purcell—contributed a large degree of his talent to playhouse music. And it fostered and appreciated excellence in acting—Thomas Betterton, Elizabeth Barry, and Anne Bracegirdle—as well as encouraged lesser players with a variety of specialized talents: Nell Gwyn, Joseph Haynes, Samuel Sandford, Susanna Percival Mountfort Verbruggen, Colley Cibber. It was a lively age, encouraging change, experimenting with the old and the new, trying out and welcoming the elements which would diversify the program and yet display the best that the drama, according to the conceptions of the age, had to offer. The audience and its taste were imperfect, of course, but they were not static. Out of their heritage, in spite of the gap created by the Puritan Commonwealth, they restored the theatres, created new and excellent dramas, kept the best of the older repertory alive, and broadened the nature of the theatrical program.

INDEX